Keep it
Country

First published 2018 by
The O'Brien Press Ltd,
12 Terenure Road East, Rathgar, D06 HD27, Dublin 6, Ireland.
Tel: +353 1 4923333; Fax: +353 1 4922777
E-mail: books@obrien.ie
Website: www.obrien.ie
The O'Brien Press is a member of Publishing Ireland.

ISBN: 978-1-84717-968-5

1 3 5 7 9 10 8 6 4 2
18 20 22 23 21 19

Printed by L&C Printing Group, Poland.
The paper in this book is produced using pulp from managed forests.

Published in:

DUBLIN
UNESCO
City of Literature

Acknowledgements

Thanks to *Sunday World* Editor Colm MacGinty, Des Gibson, Group Tabloid Editor (INM) and Jane Last, Head of News (INM), for their support; and to all the country music artists, bands, managers, road crews, photographers and publicists who helped along the way.

Photo credits

Cover photographs: Mike Denver, Cliona Hagan and Lisa McHugh photographs courtesy of Sharpe Music; Philomena Begley photograph courtesy of H&H Music; Sandy Kelly and Robert Mizzell photographs by Owen Breslin; other publicity pictures used with artists' permission.

Owen Breslin: pages 1, 3 (top right), 4, 11 (right middle), 15 (all), 18 (top left), 19 (top right), 20 (all), 21 (bottom left, bottom right), 22 (bottom right), 23 (top right), 24 (bottom left, bottom middle), 25 (right middle), 26 (bottom left, bottom right), 27 (right), 28 (left, bottom right), 29 (top left), 30 (bottom left, bottom right), 31 (middle), 32 (bottom left, bottom right), 33 (bottom left), 34, 35 (left middle, bottom left, bottom right), 36 (bottom left, bottom middle), 37 (bottom left), 38 (top left, bottom middle), 39 (bottom right), 40 (top left, bottom right) 43 (bottom left, bottom right), 46 (top right, bottom right), 47 (all), 50 (bottom), 52 (bottom right), 53 (bottom left), 57 (bottom left), 58 (bottom second from left), 60 (middle left & right) 61 (top) 62 (all), 63 (all), 64 (bottom right), 65, 66 (bottom left), 67 (both), 69 (middle left, middle right), 73 (middle right), 74, 75 (all), 77 (left middle, bottom left), 84 (middle right), 85 (both), 86 (bottom left, bottom right), 92 (right), 93 (left), 94 (right); Kevin McNulty: pages 2-3 (middle top), 12 (right top, right middle, right bottom), 18 (bottom left, middle, & right), 22 (bottom left) , 23 (bottom right), 25 (top right), 35 (top right), 38 (bottom left), 42 (top), page 55 (top left), 57 (bottom right), 70 (bottom left, second from left), 91 (bottom right), 94 (left); INM archive: pages 8 (bottom left, middle), 12 (left middle, left bottom), 13 (top left), 29 (left middle), 53 (middle right, bottom right), 55 (top right, left middle), 58 (left second from top), 60 (bottom), 73 (top right), 78 (left top, left second from top, bottom left); Philomena Begley/H&H Music: page 9 (all); Independent News and Media: (Gerry Mooney) page 10 (top), (David Conachy) pages 11 (right bottom), (Tony Gavin) page 93 (right), 95 (bottom right); Val Sheehan: pages 10 (bottom), 13 (top right), 64 (bottom left); Ritz Records: page 11 (left, right top); Sunday World: pages 54 (bottom left, bottom right), 77 (right middle, bottom right); TG4: pages 89 (all), 79 (bottom left), 44 (top left); publicity pictures used with artists' permission: pages 2 (top left), 2-3 (bottom middle), 3, 6, 7 (both), 16 (top, bottom), 19 (top left, right middle, bottom left), 21 (middle right), 23 (top left), 24 (middle left, bottom right), 25 (top left, bottom right), 26 (top left, top right), 27 (bottom left), 28 (bottom left), 29 (right), 30 (middle right), 31 (top left, bottom right), 32 (top right, middle), 33 (right, bottom middle), 36 (main pic), 37 (bottom middle, bottom right), 38 (bottom right), 39 (main pic), 40 (bottom left), 41 (both), 42 (bottom left, bottom right), 43 (right middle, bottom middle), 44 (bottom left, middle), 45 (both), 46 (bottom left), 48, 49, 50 (top), 52 (main pic), 55 (right middle, bottom middle), 56 (both), 58 (top left, bottom second from right), 59 (right second from top, right second from bottom, bottom left, bottom middle), 69 (bottom), 70 (bottom middle, bottom right), 71, 73 (top left, bottom left, bottom right), 76 (all), 78 (left top, left second from bottom), 80 (all), 81 (all), 82, 83 (all), 86 (top left), 87 (middle right, bottom middle, bottom right), 91 (bottom left), 92 (left), 95 (left, right middle), 96 (middle right, bottom middle, bottom right).

Keep it Country

A CELEBRATION OF IRISH COUNTRY MUSIC

Eddie Rowley
photo editor Owen Breslin

THE O'BRIEN PRESS
DUBLIN

Contents

The Legends
– Where It All Began

Big Tom and The Mainliners, Larry Cunningham, Margo and Philomena Begley were the leading artists who established the genre of 'Country and Irish' music in the 1960s, and popularised country throughout Ireland.

BIG TOM

'We didn't take it seriously at the start at all, y'know,' Big Tom told me, looking back on the early days of The Mainliners.

'We were playing for the fun of it, round small dance halls. We never thought it would come to anything really big.'

It was a song called 'Gentle Mother' that turned him into an Irish country superstar.

'Gentle Mother' took on a life of its own after The Mainliners performed it on 'The Showband Show' on Irish television in 1966.

Thanks to the huge success of the song in Ireland, Tom and The Mainliners were overnight sensations.

'I was astonished and a little bit scared,' Tom said, as he remembered the massive crowds that began turning up at their performances.

Gentle giant Tom McBride revealed that he was given the moniker 'Big Tom' during his days as a footballer with his local club, Oram.

The name stuck, and it served him well in showbusiness. Tom, who sadly died earlier this year, also enjoyed the title 'Ireland's King of Country'.

FACTFILE
• Tom left school at fourteen and spent five years working on his family farm, before emigrating to Scotland at the age of nineteen.
• Around that time, Tom bought a guitar, and began singing at parties.
• Tom didn't enjoy his status as a star at the height of his fame. 'It used to get to me,' he said of the recognition. 'But I got used to it and eventually accepted it. It was a small price to pay [for success].'
• Away from the stage, Tom was a farmer all his life, and he kept a collection of vintage tractors. 'I have a few of them around the farm, and I make them all work,' he said.

LARRY CUNNINGHAM

LARRY CUNNINGHAM

In 2012, Irish country music lost one of its distinctive voices and great characters with the passing of much-loved singer Larry Cunningham.

The legendary performer from County Longford left a remarkable legacy in his wake, including becoming the first Irish star to perform on 'Top Of The Pops'. This was in 1964, when he made it onto the British charts with the country hit single 'Tribute to Jim Reeves'.

Larry's signature songs, like 'Lovely Leitrim' and 'Among the Wicklow Hills', were also huge hits that particularly resonated with Irish emigrants around the world.

In 1963, Larry was asked to support Jim Reeves on a tour of Ireland. During a show in Lifford, County Donegal, Reeves walked off the stage and refused to return, because the piano in the venue was in a state of disrepair and out of tune.

There were fears that a riot was about to ensue, then Larry Cunningham came out and performed an hour of Jim Reeves' hits, leaving the crowd shouting for more. After the media picked up the story, Larry became an overnight sensation as 'Ireland's answer to Jim Reeves'.

In the mid-1970s, Larry was still topping the charts, teaming up with home-grown country and Irish sensation Margaret O'Donnell, aka Margo.

Both were then at the peak of their solo careers.

'We recorded Mr Peters, and a song called "As Soon As I Hang Up The Phone", and they were smash hits,' Margo recalls today.

FACTFILE
• Thanks to his sisters Breda and Anna, living in America and Australia, Larry received new songs in the post that weren't readily available in Ireland.
• He learned off Jim Reeves' repertoire, and could hit the low notes without any difficulty.
• He had a massive Irish hit in 1965 with 'Lovely Leitrim'. It stayed at number one in the charts for four weeks, and sold 250,000 copies.
• He was the first Irish country singer to play at New York's famous Carnegie Hall.

MARGO

Margaret O'Donnell, aka Margo, was a schoolgirl singer who became a superstar at home and abroad, striking a chord with Irish emigrants in particular during the 1960s and 1970s.

'I remember playing places like Queens in New York and singing songs like "The Hills Of Glenswilly", "Destination Donegal" and "Any Tipperary Town",' she recalls.

'People were standing thirty and forty rows deep in front of the stage, and a lot of them were crying, because it was their link with home. You were taking them back home in song.'

Margo is thrilled to have established a personal friendship with American country legend Dolly Parton.

The Donegal woman has also recorded duets with Dolly, including 'God's Colouring Book'.

'I couldn't say enough nice things about Dolly,' Margo says. 'She was great to me, and is a very positive person to be around. And anything Dolly said she would do for me, she always did.'

Despite her showbiz success, Margo's life has given her many challenges, including a personal battle with alcohol that she ultimately overcame.

One of her partners, fellow musician and singer Tony Tracey, died from cancer. 'After Tony died, I signed off on marriage,' she says. 'It's lonely sometimes on your own, but I don't dwell on it, and I have great friends.'

PHILOMENA BEGLEY

'Singing keeps me young at heart, because I enjoy it,' Philomena says. 'It's a bit of craic.'

Her love of performing for more than five decades helped Philomena deal with the less glamorous side of the business.

'It was rough on the road in the early days,' she reflects. 'You had to change into stage outfits in a toilet, or in the back of a van. The facilities were fairly primitive, especially at the marquee dances.'

Philomena famously tried to dissuade Daniel O'Donnell from going into show-business. 'I'll never forget that day,' she recalls. 'Daniel called unexpectedly to my house, and I remember that I was pregnant with my first child, Mary. I had rollers in my hair and I was up to my elbows in flour, baking bread.

'Daniel told me he was leaving college to go into the band business. I told him to "stick with the education and go for the band afterwards". At that time, it wasn't an easy business to be in. But Daniel had already made up his mind.'

FACTFILE

- At the age of fifteen, Philomena went to work in a factory that made men's hats, earning £3 and 10 shillings a week.
- In 1962, Philomena landed her first singing job, with the Old Cross Céili Band.
- After seven years in the hat factory, Philomena got her father's permission to leave the day job and become a full-time singer with the band Country Flavour.
- With her group, Philomena Begley and Her Ramblin' Men, she enjoyed a smash hit with the song 'Blanket on the Ground', which had been a chart-topper in America for Billie Jo Spears.
- Philomena made a big impact recording and touring with one of Ireland's greatest country singers, Ray Lynam, in the 1970s. Their collection of duets included their big hit, 'My Elusive Dreams'.

Daniel O'Donnell

'If there is one thing that I set out to do through my career, it was to have my place in the history of music, and that is something I have achieved. It is personally rewarding for me, as it gives me a sense of worth and well-being. I am eternally grateful to all the people who helped me to get this status. It may be a selfish thought, but there is a feelgood factor in knowing that I have made my mark and no matter what happens in the future, it is something that can never be taken from me.'

'I hope I'm growing old gracefully. I'm starting to get a bit grey. A relative spotted a few grey hairs one time, and asked me if I'd stopped dyeing my hair. But the truth is, I've never had to dye my hair. I've been very lucky to have kept my natural colour for so long.

'I'm more conscious of my appearance than the ordinary person on the street, and I guess it's because I'm in showbusiness. I work on looking as good as I can. I think the main thing that ages you is weight, either too little or too much.'

'They say home is where the heart is, and my heart has never left Donegal. There is just something magical about my native county; it has a grip on me and won't let go.'

FACTFILE

• From the age of nine, Daniel worked in a local store called The Cope. He says: 'It was my first introduction to dealing with people I'd never met before. I was always very reserved, but working in The Cope gave me the ability to reach out, and it helped me to converse well with strangers.'

• The Mullaghduff Fife and Drum Band was one of Daniel's early outings in the spotlight. 'I couldn't play anything, so they gave me the job of carrying the flag,' he laughs.

• Back in 1979, Daniel also secured a summer job digging drains in his local area. 'I hated every minute of it; it was like working on a chain gang.'

• Daniel met his wife, Majella, on holiday in Tenerife. Today they own a home on the sun-kissed isle. 'We love the climate, and the fact that we spend long periods there means that if we get a few bad days, it's not the end of the world,' he says.

• He is a fan of the nightlife in Tenerife. 'We go to the bars and love the live entertainment they offer,' he says. 'You will find us in places like The Hole In The Wall, The Irish Fiddler, Temple Bar, The Chieftain and The Dubliner, and invariably I'll get up to sing on the night.'

Above right (left to right): former manager Sean Reilly, Daniel, current manager Kieran Cavanagh, Eddie Rowley.
Right: Daniel with his wife Majella.

One of Daniel's favourite ways to escape from the world and relax with his wife, Majella, is to take a cruise holiday.

'I have been on different cruises, and I've loved every one of them. When I get up in the morning, I love the fact that I have nothing to do only organise my day the way I want.'

In January 2016, Daniel and Majella headed off on the trip of a lifetime, taking a world cruise, a treat they had promised each other after Majella had successfully undergone treatment for breast cancer.

'The sights we saw, the people we met and the different cultures we experienced is something we will never forget. We will probably never do anything on that scale again, but we will definitely go on more cruises. It really is a lovely way to spend a holiday.'

Away from the stage, Daniel is a keen golfer. 'I find that golf is a great way to relax,' he says. 'You don't have anything on your mind only the ball and the next shot when you're playing.'

Daniel took up golf by chance – a friend in Liverpool died, and his wife gave Daniel her beloved husband's golf clubs as a gift.

'I'm so bad at sport I wouldn't be allowed on to a supporters' bus, but I thought out of respect I should try out the clubs,' Daniel says. 'As frustrating as that game is, I fell in love with it. I'll never be Rory McIlroy; my golf handicap is 22 – it's nearly my age! – but I honestly enjoy it, especially when I'm playing at my local, Cruit Island.'

Daniel's favourite pastime is card playing, particularly whist. 'When I'm at home, I play cards in the hall in Kincasslagh every Tuesday night,' he reveals.

'If I had to choose things to do, that would be my favourite thing. Somebody told me that the first time they played cards with me was in 1973, when I was just about eleven. And I'm playing whist ever since.'

Daniel's success, he says, is down to finding the right people to guide his career. The man who steered his career from the very start was Sean Reilly, who was side-by-side with Daniel through good times and bad, right up to 2015.

Sean worked in Ireland with one of the country's most respected and successful promoters and managers, Kieran Cavanagh.

When Sean retired, Daniel says he feels blessed that Kieran agreed to take over the management of his career.

'Kieran has been with me since I did my first concert at the Gaiety Theatre in Dublin, back in 1988,' Daniel says. 'For me, the most important thing in every aspect of my life is to be happy and content with people, and I have a fantastic relationship with Kieran. Kieran does everything to the highest standard, and ensures that the people who spend money to come to my shows are treated well.'

The Golden Trio – Declan Nerney, Mick Flavin and John Hogan

When Daniel O'Donnell blazed a trail through the country music scene in the mid-1980s, the excitement he created opened doors for a new batch of artists, headed up by Declan Nerney, John Hogan and Mick Flavin.

DECLAN NERNEY

Starting out on the music scene while still in his teens, Longford man Declan Nerney caught the end of the glory days of the showbands.

'The big ballrooms were still going,' Declan says. 'I played places like The Casino in Castlereagh, The Majestic in Mallow and The Pavesi in Donegal town. All those venues were packed in those days. I remember how there were 2,300 people in Ardboe Hall in County Tyrone on Christmas night in 1974.

'I grew up on the showbands, so it was a great thrill for me to be doing that circuit. It was coming to the end of the showband era, but at least I got a taste of it before it died away.'

After his time with Gene Stuart in the early days of his glittering career, Declan joined another legendary band – Brian Coll and The Buckaroos.

'I played lead and steel guitar with Brian, as well as singing,' he says. 'I started singing more country and Irish songs, as Brian Coll was concentrated on country, so I had to learn more songs. They were some of the best days of my life.'

One of Declan's big hits was a song called 'The Marquee in Drumlish', which he co-wrote with Henry McMahon of The Mainliners.

Several decades later, life came full circle for Declan when he performed at a Drumlish marquee dance with one of his idols, Big Tom.

MICK FLAVIN

Mick Flavin recalls that Big Tom was one of the Irish country legends who inspired him to become an entertainer.

The Longford man once cycled twenty miles with a group of friends to see Tom perform at a carnival dance, in a place called Cornageeha.

'I had been a huge fan ever since I'd heard his big hit "Gentle Mother", while I was going to the tech in Ballinamuck in 1966.

'That night at the carnival in Cornageeha, it was so exciting to experience a live performance of Big Tom and The Mainliners. The atmosphere was incredible. It was in a huge, six-pole marquee, and it was absolutely stuffed.'

When Mick recorded his first album, *My Kind Of Country*, in 1986, he approached Daniel O'Donnell for support.

'Daniel was flying on the scene at the time, and I went along to his dance in the Park House Hotel in Edgeworthstown to meet him,' he reveals.

'I told him about my album, and how I was hoping to make a career in music. I remember getting him to record a message on a tape recorder that I had with me.

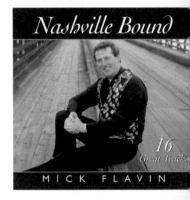

'On it, Daniel said: "This is Daniel O'Donnell, and I'd like to tell you about a new cassette my friend Mick Flavin has out. It's called *My Kind Of Country and Irish* … and it's going to be your kind of country and Irish too.' I got all the pirate radio stations to play the message at the time. And that was the start of my career.'

Mick with US country legend Buck Owens.

FACTFILE

• Mick has fond memories of his childhood growing up in a thatched farmhouse in Ballinamuck, County Longford. 'Working on a farm and running wild through the fields was a favourite part of my childhood,' he says.

• He recalls that there was an old record player in the family home, and albums by Buddy Holly, Eddie Cochran, Hank Williams and Tex Ritter. 'On my way to the well to fetch water when I was a kid, I always held the bucket over my head so I could hear the reverberation of the sound while I sang,' he reveals.

• Mick's first guitar cost the princely sum of £4, and he learned to play it from a Guitar Tutor he bought in Denniston's music shop in Longford town.

• Mick's first job was working with Longford County Council as a carpenter, and he sang part-time by night before turning professional.

• Mick was thrilled when his native county honoured him with a 'Longford Person of the Year' award for his contribution to music.

JOHN HOGAN

John Hogan credits Daniel O'Donnell with boosting the country dancing scene, leading the way for other singers like himself back in the 1980s.

John reveals that Daniel was personally supportive of his career in the early days. 'First of all, Daniel sowed the seeds for the rebirth of the live music business in Ireland after the end of the showband era,' Hogan reflects.

'He introduced me to his record label, Ritz Records, and to people who were influential in the business at the time. He was generous with his time and generous with his contacts.'

John first met Daniel when he was starting his career in 1987, after taking a gamble by spending his mortgage money to realise his dream of working as a professional singer.

John had been employed as a supervisor with Bord na Mona in Tullamore, County Offaly. He often took his guitar to work and entertained his workmates with his singing.

John was persuaded to make a record, and he recorded a song called 'Brown Eyes', which had been taught to him by his mother.

The song became an Irish Top 10 hit, making him a top attraction overnight.

John packed in his job at the briquette factory, formed a band and then went on to enjoy a massive hit with his album, *Feelings For You*.

In 1996, John was forced to give up singing for seven years on medical advice, after an undiagnosed ear problem affected his voice. He was devastated and went through tough times financially.

'At one point, I was doubtful if I could actually get back to what I love doing, and that is singing,' he says.

FACTFILE
• Born in Kilbeggan, County Westmeath, John has been living in Croghan, County Offaly, for more than thirty years.
• As well as his covers of country standards, John is a talented songwriter who has enjoyed hits with his original recordings, including 'My Feelings For You', 'Turn Back the Years', 'My Guitar', 'Irish Home' and 'Stepping Stone'.
• John was surprised to discover that his song 'Stepping Stone' was a big hit in St Lucia, where he is now treated like a superstar, and has been honoured with the freedom of the Caribbean island.
• In 1993, John recorded an album in Nashville, which included the hit 'Stepping Stone'.
• Foster & Allen have recorded several of John's songs, including 'Candlelight and Wine' and 'My Christmas'.

Lisa McHugh

Like many entertainers, Lisa McHugh reveals that she becomes larger than life when she hits the stage. 'Mum and Dad and people around me would say I'm a completely different person when I'm on stage,' Lisa says.

'Away from the spotlight, I'm a very quiet, shy person. But when I'm performing I turn a switch when I go on, because no one wants to watch a person on stage who is shy – that's boring. People want to see a show. But I'm not someone who wants to be the centre of attention off stage.'

Lisa dated Nathan Carter in the early stages of her career. She was then twenty-two, with Nathan two years younger. 'We met at an awards show in Antrim,' Lisa reveals. 'We were both away from home and starting off in the business, so we had that in common straight away. After that night, we stayed in touch, became friends and were very much a support for each other.'

Their friendship soon developed into a romance. 'We were seeing each other for a while. After several months, it came to a point where we were both so busy with our careers, we never really saw each other, so we decided to go our separate ways. It did us no harm at all, as we are still the best of friends.'

DOWN ON THE FARM

Lisa has fond memories of her childhood. 'I grew up on a small farm outside Glasgow. It wasn't a huge working farm, but there were cattle, pigs, sheep and a couple of horses. I loved the outdoor life, and still do. I'd been out among the animals feeding them, and I loved being on the horses.'

FACTFILE

• Lisa was born in Glasgow, but her mum is from Falcarragh, County Donegal, and her dad is a native of Castlederg, County Tyrone.

• She taught herself to sing in a hall at the back of her home. 'I would sing for hours to myself,' she reveals, adding that Dolly Parton and Martina McBride were among her favourite American singers.

• Lisa's most treasured possession is a guitar she got from her parents for her twenty-first birthday.

• Lisa developed a national profile when she performed as a contestant on 'Glór Tíre' on TG4 in 2009, mentored by Robert Mizzell. 'You couldn't buy the kind of publicity I got out of that show,' she says.

• Lisa later appeared on 'Glór Tíre' as a mentor to singer Grainne Gavigan.

• Daniel O'Donnell played a major role in Lisa's early success. 'I'll always be grateful to Daniel, as he was very supportive of me when I started out, and duetted with me on my Christmas single, "I'll Be Home With Bells On".'

• Although born in Liverpool, Nathan has Irish connections. His great-grandmother was from Newry.

• After leaving school, Nathan worked as a labourer with his father, Ian, while trying to establish his singing career.

• At the age of seventeen, he moved to Ireland, where the country music scene was thriving. He joined a band formed by well-known Irish songwriter and singer John Farry.

• He credits his grandmother, Ann McCoy, with helping him to launch his career. Described as 'his secret weapon', Ann got him gigs in his native Liverpool, and was his driver in the early days. Today, Ann can be found selling merchandise at his shows.

• Working on the pub scene in Liverpool taught Nathan tough lessons, like how to deal with a rowdy crowd. 'After working on that scene you can handle most things,' he says. 'There were a few nights that were hairy, with people fighting in front of me.'

• Nathan will never forget his last performance in the UK before he moved to Ireland. It was the summer of 2008, and he was one of the acts chosen to perform at the historic closing of the famous Galtymore ballroom in London's Cricklewood, where Big Tom topped the bill. 'To be the opening act for Big Tom and getting the chance to play the Galtymore before it closed was a major deal for me,' he says.

Nathan Carter

FAVOURITE CHILDHOOD MEMORY

'Playing at the Fleadh Cheoil in Listowel when I was about eleven, and sneaking into every pub in the town to perform a few tunes. My biggest thrill was winning the All Ireland traditional singing at the Fleadh.'

MOST EMBARRASSING MOMENT

'I fell into a piano on stage when I was a ten-year-old kid in a choir, which was very embarrassing. I was the last one walking out on stage, and I tripped and ended up in the piano. Not my finest moment.'

Nathan remembers that he stumbled on his biggest hit, 'Wagon Wheel', by chance. 'A friend of mine had the original version, by the American band Old Crow Medicine Show, as a ring tone on his phone,' Nathan explains.

'Every time it rang I thought it was very annoying, but at the same time it was very catchy. I then went into the studio and recorded it with my own arrangement.

'Then I made a video for it with some friends, and that was a lot of fun to do. We made it on Rossnowlagh beach in Donegal, but there was no glamour in it. It was a freezing cold day, and it took ten of us to lift a piano on to the beach for the performance.'

The 'Wagon Wheel' video was an instant hit for Nathan. 'It got 300,000 views in the first month, and the most I had before that was 80,000 in a year.'

Right: Nathan with Liverpool football legend John Aldridge

Nathan always says he was built for the road. It's a tough life, but being a single man with no children, he can enjoy it. 'I'm happiest when I'm on the road performing,' he says. 'Probably eighty per cent of my year revolves around gigging and touring, whether it's making CDs or doing TV or playing the shows.'

In March 2018, Nathan played to nearly 15,000 people, between the 3Arena in Dublin and SSE Arena in Belfast. It was Nathan's second year in succession to perform in both arenas, and he said the novelty of seeing his name up in lights at those venues will never wear off. He also loved the fact that his family, including his parents and grandparents, were around to experience those spectacular events in his career.

'Of course, playing those venues would be pointless if there were no fans, so a big thank you to everyone who makes the effort to come and see me.'

One of the highlights of Nathan's 2018 has been seeing his kid brother, Jake, win Ireland's 'Dancing With The Stars'.

'None of us expected when Jake went into DWTS that he'd be so good, but it transpires that, unlike me, he's a natural when it comes to dancing,' Nathan laughs.

'Of course, you get nothing for nothing in this life, and he really put in the time and work, along with his professional dance partner Karen Byrne, to master all those incredible dances he performed throughout the series.

'The Irish public love Karen, and rightly so, because she is one of life's incredible people. Karen has worked hard for what she has achieved. She is so talented, but most of all, Karen has a heart of gold.'

Nathan's favourite holiday destinations are Las Vegas and the Mexican resort of Cancun.

'There is such a great buzz in Las Vegas,' he says. 'I mainly go to watch the shows, and in recent years I've seen Elton John, Celine Dion, George Strait and Kacey Musgraves performing there.'

Nathan insists that he's not a big gambler. 'I do love the casinos, they're really good fun, but I try not to go too mad in them.'

He goes to Cancun to top up his tan. 'Cancun is the most idyllic place to have a relaxing holiday. I love the sun and enjoy water-sports, so when I'm not sunbathing you'll find me jet-skiing, water skiing and paragliding.'

Mike Denver

MIKE'S PIPE DREAM

'Before I became a full-time country singer, I did an apprenticeship as a plumber. My mother and father wanted me to have something to fall back on if the singing didn't work out. They said, "Look, follow your dream, but there could be lean times with the singing, so give yourself an option." At seventeen, I got a job and served my time as a plumber.'

THE LOVE OF LIZ

'Walking down the aisle has been the best moment of my life,' Mike reveals. 'I first met my wife, Liz, when she brought her mother to see one of my concerts in Westmeath. We got chatting afterwards and hit it off. It takes a special kind of person to live with somebody who is in this business, and fortunately I found that person in Liz.'

As a young boy, Mike Denver was captivated by the recordings of American and Irish greats George Jones and Big Tom.

'The twists and turns of life are very strange all right,' Mike reflects today. 'Big Tom and George Jones were the guys on the radio and on television when I was growing up. Never for a moment did I think I would get to be a part of their world.

'I had the unbelievable luck to record a song with George Jones in Nashville. When I saw George arriving into the studio, my legs went to jelly. The man was country music royalty, and there was something about him that is indescribable. I was in total awe of him, but he was a gentleman to work with.'

A total professional, Mike says he takes care of his health with regular gym exercise, and is conscious of his stage appearance and style of clothing. 'At the very beginning, my image was the cowboy hat and white suit, but I moved with the times and now have a more modern look.'

FACTFILE

• The country star who made the biggest impression on Mike in his youth was Garth Brooks. 'My favourite country song is "The Dance",' he reveals.

• Mike fondly remembers his first night as a professional singer. 'It was in the Park House Hotel in Edgeworthstown, County Longford, and the first song I sang was "Country Roads". You never forget the first night, and it's still a thrill thinking back on it.'

• Mike is dedicated to his role as an entertainer. 'I wouldn't say I'm insecure, but I'm always striving to be better at what I do. I'm my own worst critic.'

• Speaking about his fans, Mike says: 'There are hardcore fans who follow me from one end of the country to the other. They take a few days off, and go from dance to dance or concert to concert. Country fans are a great bunch of people.'

FACTFILE

• Michael's early influences were Andy Williams and Matt Monroe. He says: 'A friend in a local record shop gave me their albums, and told me it was the music I should be listening to. I fell in love with them immediately.'

• The 'X Factor' judge Louis Walsh guided his career for a short time. 'Louis gave me great belief in myself,' he reveals.

• Margo O'Donnell is one of Michael's favourite singers. He wrote a song for Margo called 'A Pocketful Of Dreams'.

• Michael was thrilled when living legend Phil Coulter agreed to produce his album, *This Is Michael English*. 'I feel Phil brought out the best in me,' he says.

Michael English

FROM RUSSIA WITH LOVE

'One of my favourite childhood memories is performing on the "Late Late Toy Show" at the age of twelve. I played a tune I composed myself. It was called "Perestroika", a Russian term I'd heard on the news at the time. My teacher told me it meant peace. The following morning, I got a phone call at home, offering me my first gig – playing relief to Dickie Rock in a very famous ballroom called Green Acres, just outside Carlow.'

MUSIC TO MY EARS

'For me, the most relaxing thing is writing music. I know nothing else, really, as I've been playing and creating music all my life. It's like an artist sitting down to paint a picture, they find it relaxing. I write for other people as well. Different types of music. That gets you away from the job and the music you do yourself.'

Michael says he's lucky to be around at a time when country music is thriving. 'Country music is like a big wheel, it keeps turning, and when it turns so much it revives itself again,' he reflects. 'There was the night-club scene, the pop scene … and country music seems to keep coming back. I've never seen it as good, ever. I think it's because in Ireland, people like a song that has a story, and country songs are story songs.'

One of Michael's biggest fans was the late Irish golf legend Christy O'Connor Jnr, who died suddenly in January 2016. 'From the moment I met him, at a charity concert fifteen years earlier, Christy became my biggest supporter,' Michael reveals. 'Christy loved all types of music, but I was the music that he really loved, and we had many, many sessions.'

Michael was one of the musicians and singers who played at Christy's funeral. 'I sang a hymn called "I Watch The Sun Rise". The chorus goes, "May I be always close to you, following all your ways".'

Derek Ryan

ON THE BALL

Sunday was a special day in Derek Ryan's childhood. 'I loved Sunday mornings when I was a young boy,' Derek recalls. 'After Mass, we'd go to play handball with friends, and then it would be home for the dinner. Then we'd play music in the house afterwards, religiously. It sounds like 'The Waltons', but that's what we used to do.'

FALLING FOR THE BELLE

'There have been a few embarrassing moments on stage. I remember performing in Blackpool one night and, as I was being introduced on to the stage, I fell going up the steps, in full view of the crowd. I really hurt myself, and I had to go on and sing "The Belle Of Liverpool" in pain.'

Derek is also an award-winning songwriter, whose songs have been recorded by other singers, including Daniel O'Donnell. 'It's a great feeling to have your songs recognised by someone like Daniel,' Derek says. 'It was a real career highlight for me when Daniel sang my song, "God's Plan", on the "Late Late Show", and then we performed it together on TG4's "Opry An Iúir". That was surreal to me.'

MY TOP FIVE ALBUMS – DEREK RYAN

1. Bryan Adams – *MTV Unplugged*
2. Keith Urban – *Greatest Hits*
3. Johnny McEvoy – *Definitive Collection*
4. Bruce Springsteen – *We Shall Overcome, Seeger Sessions*
5. Michael Bublé – *Crazy Love*

FACTFILE

- It was seeing Garth Brooks performing in Croke Park in 1997 that fuelled Derek's ambition to become an entertainer. 'Garth made country cool, and there was an amazing atmosphere,' he says.
- A favourite musical memory for Derek was winning the All Ireland céilí drumming in the 1998 Fleadh Cheoil in Enniscorthy. 'It was a pretty tough competition, so I was delighted to win it,' he says. 'I retired then, so I got out at the top!'
- Derek's father played a major role in fostering his love of music. 'Daddy would have always softly pushed us into music,' he says. 'He played music, and when we were young we'd sneak into his gigs during the summer.'
- For a period in the early Noughties, Derek was a pop idol in boyband D-Side. 'I got into pop, because at the time it was every young guy's dream, after the success of Boyzone,' he says. 'But what I'm doing now was always my ultimate plan.'
- Whenever he gets a break from performing, Derek's favourite place to relax in Ireland with his wife is in Killarney. 'We go for a lot of walks in the national park, and rent bikes and go cycling. At night there are great places to eat and, of course, lots of entertainment.'

Let's Go Jiving

TOP CHOREOGRAPHER GERARD BUTLER ON THE DANCING CRAZE THAT HAS SET THE DANCEHALLS ALIGHT

WHERE DID JIVING START IN IRELAND?

'Nobody knows the origin of the jive in Ireland. But a guy called Jimmy Gralton returned home from the States to his native Effernagh, County Leitrim, during the Depression in the 1920s. He opened a dance hall, where he started to teach some of the jive dances from America, and share his socialist views.

'The Catholic Church and the State wasn't impressed, because they had no control over what was going on in the hall, so ultimately they got him deported. He's the only Irishman who was extradited out of Ireland for dancing!'

Gralton's story was made into a 2014 movie called *Jimmy's Hall*.

'My father remembers that the first jive he ever saw was in 1964, at a marquee dance in Croghan village, County Roscommon. A couple from Carrick-on-Shannon came home from London where they had been living. They had learned how to jive in London, and when they started jiving in the marquee that night, the whole place stopped to look at them.'

HOW DIFFICULT IS IT TO LEARN A JIVE?

'I can teach a guy or girl to jive in fifteen minutes if he or she has the ability.'

WHAT'S THE THRILL OF A JIVE?

'This applies to dancing in general: Once you hit a venue for two hours, no matter what pressures you have in your life, they're forgotten for those couple of hours. You are in a different zone. It's a real tonic, and it becomes a drug in a way.'

DID YOU ALWAYS HAVE A PASSION FOR DANCING?

'I loved going to the social dances and doing jiving when I was sixteen and seventeen. I really stuck out, because everybody else was in their forties, fifties and sixties. I had a different style of dancing, and threw in a few rock'n'roll moves. My mother would give me a look sometimes, as if to say, "Stop showing off." Through word of mouth, I got asked to teach a move here, and a move there, and then I started workshops.'

'At first it was all girls at the dance classes, but then the guys realised that to engage with the girls on a dance floor, they'd have to learn to jive as well. At a recent dance class, I had more men than women!'

FACTFILE
• Gerard, from Boher, County Roscommon, started dancing at a young age, having been taught céilí and set dancing by his father, Seamus, and social dancing by his late mother, Lila.
• Gerard holds nine All-Ireland titles for different styles of dance.
• Having left school at sixteen, he went to work as a trainee storeman in a garage by day, and taught dancing by night.
• He toured internationally for three years as a dancer and percussionist with the show 'Rhythm of the Dance'.

FACTFILE

• One of Jimmy's earliest memories is of singing in an old, deserted dancehall, The Crystal, situated at the back of his family's pub in Doon, County Limerick. 'I'd get up on the stage and sing, imagining that there was a huge audience out in front of me.'

• As a youngster, Jimmy would go singing with the 'wren boys' at Christmas time. 'Myself and a cousin, Tom, would do the pubs, then change into different costumes and go back and do the same pubs. It was very profitable,' he laughs.

• He first came to national prominence when he won the RTÉ television talent show 'Secrets', which was presented by the late Gerry Ryan.

• A song called 'Your Wedding Day', written by his then-manager Henry McMahon of The Mainliners, gave Jimmy his first major hit in this country.

• He achieved every country singer's dream when he recorded a duet, 'The Grand Tour', with the late American legend George Jones. 'George was to country what Elvis was to rock'n'roll, so it doesn't get much better than that,' says Jimmy.

Jimmy Buckley

Jimmy Buckley remembers getting a quick lesson on the ups and downs of life in the music business shortly after launching his first band.

'My first night as a country artist got off to a reasonably good start,' Jimmy recalls. 'That first gig was in Doon Hall, County Limerick, where I come from, and you couldn't move in the place.

'The following night, we went up to Roscommon to play The Four Ps in Rathallen, and we had twenty-seven people at the dance. I struggled on from week to week and month to month, and sometimes my parents would have to supplement me to pay the band.'

One of Jimmy's first band wagons was a Mercedes van that had previously been owned by the 'King of Country', Big Tom.

'There was huge mileage on the van, so it was always breaking down,' Jimmy says. 'It was insured as a fruit and veg van, because you couldn't get musician insurance then.

'We were driving along one day and a stone broke the windscreen. Me and my roadie, a fella called Speedy, spent the next couple of days driving with duffle coats on us, because I hadn't the money for a new windscreen.'

Some years ago, Jimmy teamed up with his pals Robert Mizzell and Patrick Feeney, to form Irish country music supergroup The Three Amigos.

'I honestly can't wait to get up on stage with Robert and Patrick, because we have the best of fun,' Jimmy says. 'There is a genuine bond between us. We enjoy each other's company, and we work well together as a group.'

Robert Mizzell

Robert Mizzell credits his foster parents, Regina and Dayton 'Blackie' Courtney, with giving him stability in his childhood and setting him on the road to a successful life.

Robert was taken into care as a child, having suffered physical abuse in the family home in Shreveport, Louisiana. 'If it wasn't for Mama and Papa Courtney, as we called them, I wouldn't have known that there is a better life out there; and I wouldn't be here today.

'The Courtneys fostered more than thirty children during their time. They gave a lot of people a great start in life.'

It was love that brought Robert to Ireland, after meeting an Irish girl in America. When she returned home to the old sod, twenty-year-old Robert came with her.

His first Irish job was working on the buildings. 'The things that happen on a building site for an Irishman are tough enough, but when you're a young American coming over here and you have no idea what "the craic" is, and you don't know what a "yoke" is, you're in trouble,' Robert laughs.

'Everyone on the job called me "Yank". One day the foreman said to me, "Yank, go down and get that yoke." I was too proud to ask what he meant as I went looking for the yoke.

'I asked one of the other lads, who pointed to a transformer for plugging in power tools. I then associated the transformer with a "yoke", so for the next three weeks, whenever anyone asked me for a yoke I handed them a transformer. It became a running joke on the site.'

'Ireland and the Irish people have given me so much to be thankful for,' Robert says. 'I have a great following of very loyal fans all over Ireland. They have even travelled with me to America, when I organised a tour to my native Shreveport. I really am grounded in this country.'

'I try to stay in good shape and keep my image up, because nobody wants to see a fat country singer,' Robert says. 'I'm enjoying the business now better than I ever did, and I feel like I'm twenty years old.'

- Before moving to Ireland, Robert served in the American army in New Haven, Connecticut. 'It's the best thing I ever did, and the hardest. It knocked the rough edges off me,' he says.

- Louis Walsh advised Robert to contact Irish showband star, songwriter and promoter Tommy Swarbrigg. Tommy set Robert on the road to stardom with an original song called 'Kickass Country'.

- He married Adele, in 2013, and the happy couple have a daughter, Maisie. Robert also has an adult daughter, Amy, from his first marriage.

- Robert is a member of The Three Amigos. 'I think the Amigos tick all the boxes for fans,' he says. 'It's got country, a little bit of light rock'n'roll, pop, some middle-of-the-road and lots of comedy.'

FACTFILE

- Patrick began his journey into the world of music playing in a two-piece band with his father, Patrick, at the age of fourteen.
- Daniel O'Donnell helped Patrick on the road to success when he invited him as a guest singer on an RTÉ show he was hosting at the time. 'That's something I'll never forget,' Patrick says.
- Patrick launched his solo career at the age of nineteen with his own band, and released seven successful albums in his twenties.
- Being one third of The Three Amigos has spread Patrick's fan base. 'I love singing, comedy and acting, and I get to do all three in the Amigos,' he says.

Patrick Feeney

Patrick Feeney combines his life as a performer with part-time farming on his forty-acre farm in Culfadda, County Sligo.

The singer breeds Limousin cattle. 'It's light farming for me, and it's like a hobby,' he says. 'My dad has an active interest in it as well, and he looks after the stock when I'm away.'

Patrick feels that farming gives him the perfect boost to help him cope with life on the road. 'I love getting into a Jeep on a Monday morning and heading out on the land,' he says.

In 2008, after ten years performing, Patrick took a year out and travelled across America.

'It was like a student year out, which I'd never done,' he explains. 'I did Route 66, and I visited places like Nashville, Memphis, Phoenix and Reno. All the things you dream about doing, I did them.'

The time out gave Patrick a new perspective on where he wanted to go with his life and career. 'Before I returned from America, I knew I was going to go back on the road,' he says.

The popular entertainer has battled through an illness that threatened to put him in a wheelchair.

In 2013, Patrick's world came crashing down when he was diagnosed with Crohn's disease, which affects the digestive system. He also has a rare form of arthritis called Ankylosing Spondylitis, which gives him pain in all his joints.

Thankfully, modern drugs and a new healthy regime have helped Patrick to cope, and to continue his life as one of Ireland's top entertainers.

'What frightened me was the day I was told that if I didn't change my lifestyle, I'd end up in a wheelchair,' he reveals.

'I did CBT (cognitive behavioural therapy) for eight weeks. It was fantastic, because it took me out of the state of mind I was in, where I was bitter and asking, "Why me?" Now I look on the positive side of things, rather than the negatives.'

'I also space out my performing over the year, and thanks to medication I live a good life.'

Cliona Hagan

From Ballinderry, County Tyrone, Cliona Hagan reached the final of 'The All Ireland Talent Show' on RTÉ television in 2009, where she was mentored by Eurovision Song Contest winner Dana.

'It was amazing how fate brought us together,' Cliona says. 'When I was in my first year in secondary school, I sang "All Kinds of Everything" in my school play. I never imagined that I'd end up working with Dana.'

IT STARTED ON 'THE LATE LATE SHOW'

Cliona will never forget her first television performance. 'It was singing "Silent Night" on "The Late Late Toy Show" at the age of twelve,' she reveals. 'Afterwards, I got a fabulous reaction from everybody at home. The neighbours and the local community were really proud. I even got a shout-out at school assembly, and everybody was clapping. Busted and S Club 7 were also on the show, and it was so cool getting to meet them.'

POETRY RECITAL WAS A HICCUP

'When I was growing up, I did speech and drama, and I remember one time reciting poetry at a feis and being so nervous that I developed a fit of hiccups. I was so embarrassed about that, but everybody started clapping for me. I thought, "Okay, this is good; if I can get through hiccuping during a poem, I can get through anything."'

Cliona sees herself as 'the new kid on the block'. She says: 'I'm just trying to do my best to make everybody in the Irish country music scene proud of me. Everybody has been so supportive – the likes of Nathan, Lisa and Derek.

'Philomena Begley has also taken me under her wing, and given me lots of great advice. I was thrilled when Daniel O'Donnell came over to me at the RTÉ Irish Country Music Awards, and told me how wonderful a singer he thought I was. That made my night. It feels like I'm part of a wee family.'

FACTFILE

- Cliona started out as a classical singer. 'I was put into the classical genre of music when I went for singing lessons at a young age, because of my high register,' she says.
- Now an award-winning country music singer, Cliona says: 'I loved classical, but with country music, I was singing in English and I could relate to it more. It just spiralled from there.'
- She grew up with a love of country. 'Whether it was American or Irish country, I loved it, with my favourites being the Dixie Chicks and Garth Brooks ... and, of course, the great Irish country singers like Daniel O'Donnell, Philomena Begley and Susan McCann.'

Dominic Kirwan

'I've had some wonderful, wonderful times. I've been able to rear my family through music. I wouldn't change my life. I wouldn't change the fact that I'm a singer and entertainer. For the world that I've experienced, the living I've had, the travelling and the people that I've met, it's been fantastic and something I wouldn't swap. But, as strange as it seems, I don't ever remember sitting down and deciding that I wanted to be a singer and performer. Things happened for me.'

Dominic says he has never become blasé about entertaining a live audience. 'The day you take what you do for granted is the day you should give it up,' he says. 'Nothing beats the feeling of stepping out on stage and bringing a show to life. You know that people have gone to a lot of effort and expense to come and see you, and it is such a great sense of achievement when you send them home happy.'

CHARLEY PRIDE

Dominic has particularly fond memories of Charley Pride from his days playing support to the American legend. 'The amazing thing about Charley Pride is that he made a point of finding out all about me before we met,' he says. 'And within two or three days of touring with him, Charley knew everyone in my band by name. He would meet them backstage and say, "Hi Seamus!" [the piano player], "Hi Tony!" [the sax player], and so on. He taught me that no matter who you are, who you are with, or where you go, you should be aware that there's always somebody there that needs a helping hand and encouragement. And without the team around you, you can't function. I still get a card from Charley every Christmas.'

FACTFILE

- Dominic's first public performance was as an Irish dancer in a feis at the tender age of six.
- Dominic started off entering local talent competitions and playing pubs, clubs and weddings around Omagh, in a band called The Melody Boys.
- After winning a minor recording contract in a competition, Dominic released his first album, *The Green Fields Of Ireland*.
- His album *Evergreen* became a big hit, with his version of 'The Answer To Everything' becoming particularly popular in the UK.
- Dominic caught the attention of Mick Clerkin of Ritz Records, where Daniel O'Donnell was the leading artist.
- Major tours followed with Philomena Begley, Charley Pride (1990) and Tammy Wynette (1991). Later, Dominic toured with Kenny Rogers and Don Williams.
- Dominic's son Colm has a degree in musical theatre and toured with *Jesus Christ Superstar*. He also toured with the late Don Williams, and is working as a songwriter in Nashville.
- His son Barry is also one of Ireland's top young country stars.

FACTFILE

• Back in 1991, aged fifteen, Johnny joined a country band with two of his uncles.

• A series of stints in different groups followed, playing everything from indie to pop and rock.

• Before returning to country music, Johnny fronted a tribute band called Raised on Rock, singing the songs of bands like Bon Jovi, Guns N' Roses and AC/DC.

• His style of country is more American than Irish, and he cites artists like Keith Urban among his influences.

• He credits his own mother with giving him a love of country. 'My mother reared me on country music,' he says, adding that she was a member of Susan McCann's fan club.

Johnny Brady

Juggling a busy music career and rearing a young family leaves no time for hobbies in Johnny Brady's world.

The man from Randalstown, County Antrim, spends long periods away from home, performing around the country.

Married with two young children – 'and two Jack Russells,' he adds – it's a tough sacrifice to make in order to pursue his career as a country star.

It was probably inevitable that Johnny would find his way into the world of country music, having been exposed to it as a child.

'I'm a second cousin of Big Tom – my grandfather and his mum were brother and sister,' Johnny reveals.

'Tom was a big figure in my life growing up,' he acknowledges. 'He had his bar, the Old Log Cabin, in Castleblayney in the 1980s, which his brother Seamus ran for him in those days.

'From the time I was four, I was able to go into the Old Log Cabin with my grandfather. Monday night was the big night there for music, and I used to sit in front of all the bands every week and watch them.

'Tom would be there an odd Monday night, and he'd get up and do a song or two with the bands.'

Big Tom encouraged Johnny to develop his love of country and to go down that route as an entertainer.

'Tom knew that I was coming from a pop background as a professional singer, but when I went to him to say I was thinking of concentrating on country music, he was very supportive.

'"There's one thing I'll say to you, Johnny – when you meet a fan in the country music scene, you have a fan for life," he told me. And that is so true.'

Susan McCann

Susan McCann, from Forkhill, County Armagh, is known as Ireland's First Lady of Country Music. She started singing in 1965 at sixteen years old, with popular local group the John Murphy Céilí Band. Romance blossomed in the band when she fell in love with the accordion player, Dennis Heaney, who has been her life-long partner and beloved husband.

'There was no country scene at the time,' Susan says. 'It was Big Tom who introduced country into his music, and then Philomena Begley and myself introduced it into the céilí scene.'

In 1977, Susan launched her career with a number one hit called 'Big Tom Is Still The King'. In Nashville, Susan's talent was spotted by Porter Wagoner, the man who launched Dolly Parton's career.

Susan made six appearances on the iconic Grand Ole Opry, and at Florida's famous Strawberry Fair she entertained two former US Presidents, George Bush Snr. and George W. Bush, as well as General 'Stormin'' Norman Schwarzkopf.

Today, Susan's greatest joy is spending time with her grandchildren. 'I missed out rearing my own, because I was on the road that much,' she says.

'I have a son and daughter. When they were bigger, I took them with us quite a bit during the holidays, and when they were at school we always travelled through the night to be with them rather than stay over after gigs. I didn't want them to grow up and say, "Our mammy was never there." And that's not how they remember it, thankfully.'

Susan with George W. Bush.

With Irish country star Brendan Quinn.

Susan and Tammy Wynette.

Ray Lynam

One of Ireland's greatest country 'voices', Ray Lynam, from Moate, County Westmeath, began his career playing saxophone in local band The Merrymen, while in secondary school.

Ray found fame as frontman with The Hillbillies in the 1970s, with their first hit a cover of the Buck Owens song 'Sweet Rosie Jones'.

Back then, Ray was a shy, unsasuming performer with a pure country voice. 'I was never really comfortable with being the frontman,' he says. 'I would have preferred to have been in the background to be honest.'

In the early days, Lynam was a pin-up idol, appearing on the cover of *Spotlight* magazine. He had the voice and talent to match the hype, but disliked the celebrity side of the business. 'That was the hard work part of it,' he laughs.

Hugely respected and with thousands of fans, Ray Lynam and The Hillbillies filled dance halls across the land. 'I was very lucky I was there in the good times,' he says today. 'And it helped that I happened to be friends with good musicians.'

During the Wembley Country Music Festival in 1974, Ray teamed up with Ireland's Queen of Country, Philomena Begley. He went on to record many hits with her, including 'My Elusive Dreams'.

In recent years, Ray and Philomena have been performing as part of Mike Denver's concert tour. 'I always look forward to meeting up with musicians and singers from the early days, although today we have to fight over parking space for our Zimmer frames,' he jokes.

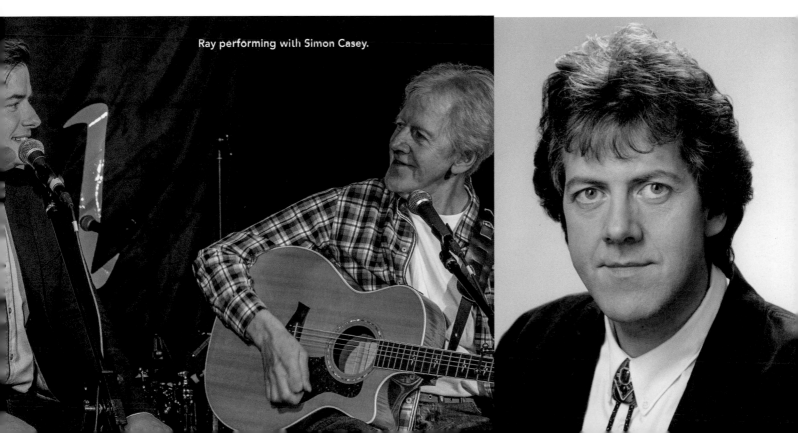

Ray performing with Simon Casey.

John McNicholl

It was Daniel O'Donnell who discovered John McNicholl's star quality as a singer.

'I used to go to the Kincasslagh festival every year, and I would sing in the church choir there with Daniel,' John explains.

'One year, Daniel told the crowd, "Folks, I think this young man here should have a band of his own, what do you think?" They all cheered and clapped. It started from there.'

'I couldn't be happier, because I've always genuinely loved this music,' he says. 'When my friends were going to night clubs, I would be going off to see live bands like Daniel, Philomena Begley, Sean O'Farrell or Kathy Durkin.

John is as famous for his stylish stage outfits as his exciting brand of entertainment.

And the singer says his love of fashion goes back to his childhood days. 'My mother used to own a clothes shop, so everyone in my family developed an interest in fashion as we grew up,' he reveals.

FACTFILE

• Born and raised in the small village of Foreglen in Derry, John is one of fifteen children.

• John's 2004 debut album, *Something Old, Something New*, became an instant hit with fans at home and in the UK.

• John hit a winning formula as a songwriter with his single 'Come On Dance'. 'It got great reviews and a huge response from fans,' he says.

• His hit singles include 'Walk Down The Aisle With Me', 'Sealed With A Kiss' and 'Dig A Little Deeper In The Well'.

Gerry Guthrie

A popular attraction on the live dancing scene around the country with his superb band, singer and guitarist Gerry Guthrie brings a lot of experience to the stage.

Gerry joined Sandy Kelly's band in 2000, spending three years performing in the major league.

'That really was a fantastic time in my life,' Gerry recalls. 'Sandy was at the peak of her career, so we were playing fabulous venues.'

Gerry's earliest recording was 'Sunday Morning Christian', a song he first heard Big Tom singing.

This track would set the talented Ballina man on the road to success – and lead to him being taken under the wing of Big Tom's band leader Henry McMahon.

'I'm being managed by a member of The Mainliners. That has given me a connection with the remarkable Irish country band. It's like being part of Irish country music history in a small way.'

Gerry grew up listening to Big Tom. 'The first time I ever heard him was in my grandmother's house in Ballina, on an old record player. I just loved his voice. I don't think there's anybody in our scene that hasn't been influenced by Big Tom and The Mainliners.'

Gerry got to know the country legend through the years. 'After Tom heard me singing one night, he said to me, "You're a true country singer." That's high praise from somebody like Big Tom.'

FACTFILE
• By the age of fifteen, Gerry was on his way to a career in music, having won his place in a local band, The New Blues, who were performing on the pub and cabaret scene.
• After his later role as a guitarist in Sandy Kelly's band, Gerry got further experience in bands fronted by Martin Cuffe, Shawn Cuddy and Louise Morrissey, before taking the leap to become a star in his own right.
• He has also won critical acclaim for his duet with Irish singer Matt Leavy on the Alan Jackson hit "Come On In".

Country Cruises and Craic on the Costas

Irish country music trips to holiday hotspots like Spain and Portugal, or across to America, have become hugely popular with home fans in recent decades.

Nathan Carter has his 'Carter on the Costa'; Jimmy Buckley hosts 'Craic on the Costa'; Michael English heads up his all-star trip; and Declan Nerney has his 'Hooley in the Sun'. All of these take place in Spain.

Robert Mizzell has whisked his fans off on a journey back to his roots in Shreveport, Louisiana.

Promoter Paul Claffey organises annual trips to the continent, with a glittering bill of Irish entertainers. He says fans love to soak up the sun while also enjoying top-class country music performers from home.

There are also Irish country cruises around the Mediterranean and the Caribbean, with major stars such as Daniel O'Donnell.

Daniel with family country band The Davitts.

DANIEL O'DONNELL

'I have been on cruise ships as a singer, and I love the lifestyle, as does Majella,' Daniel says. 'Before I went on a cruise for the first time, I wasn't sure if I would enjoy it, but you are treated like royalty on board. I have since been on different cruises, both professionally and personally, and loved every one of them.

'I have also worked with a lady called Gertrude Byrne, who runs an "All Star Irish Cruise" in the Caribbean every year, and I have been one of the performers. That is a week-long cruise with other entertainers, and it's always so much fun. From my point of view, it allowed me the opportunity to go and see the other Irish singers and performers, which is something I love to do, but don't normally get the chance to when I'm working.

'The cruise stops at various ports by day, so you can go exploring different cities and locations. But if you don't want to leave the ship, there are so many activities on board that you'll never be bored. And, of course, you can just spend the time relaxing around the pool in the sun, like you would in a holiday resort. At night, the variety of entertainment is incredible. People go back time after time on those cruises.

'Outside of work, Majella and I have gone on many cruises with our friends. We also did a world cruise together after Majella recovered from breast cancer, and that was one of the best experiences of our lives.'

DOMINIC KIRWAN

'What I love about the cruises is that it gives you the opportunity to interact with other entertainers,' says Dominic. 'I was on a recent cruise with Daniel O'Donnell, and it was great to sit down and catch up with him for a proper chat. I have a great relationship with Daniel. I can confide in him and I know the conversation will go no further. We have always got on well together, and have a lot of mutual respect.

'From the fans' point of view, a cruise or a music holiday in the sun is the chance to spend a week with their favourite artists and enjoy music morning, noon and night, while the artists get to hang out together and see each other perform.'

CARTER ON THE CRUISE

'People always say that they leave a cruise with fabulous memories, and that is certainly true in my case,' Nathan says.

'Two questions I'm often asked about cruises are, "Do you not get bored on the ship?" and, "Is it very rocky?" The answer to both questions is, "No."

'The beautiful cruise ships are like a floating city, and you don't realise that it's moving. There is so much to do on board, with tennis courts, gyms, indoor and outdoor swimming pools, numerous group and individual activities, and all kinds of entertainment, from pop and jazz to country music, in the theatres and bars.

'On my last Caribbean cruise, with entertainers that included American country legend Charley Pride and Engelbert Humperdinck, I took the opportunity to explore some of the islands, including St Thomas and Caicos, that we visited along the route, and I soaked up the sun every day while relaxing in a hot tub. It doesn't get much better than that, particularly at the start of the year when the weather is so bad back home.'

CARTER ON THE COSTA

'If you're into country music or folk music, once you've gone on one of those trips, a normal holiday seems a bit dull, because you've got music going on from early afternoon into the early hours of the morning. There's dancing, there's craic, there's singalongs and sessions; you can't really go wrong if you're into music, which a lot of people are. It's like a festival of your favourite artists performing all week.

'I have twelve acts on my "Carter on the Costa" trip this year. Imagine what you'd pay to see twelve acts at home every day. Plus, when you do an outdoor festival in Ireland, you never know what the weather is going to be like, but on foreign trips you are guaranteed the sun or a balmy climate … and a jug of sangria!'

Jim Devine

Jim Devine shot to fame when he appeared as a contestant on the RTÉ television talent show 'The Voice of Ireland' in 2012.

The Tyrone man had been playing the pubs and clubs for years when he decided to chance his luck on 'The Voice'.

Fortunately, the chairs turned for him. He was snapped up by Kian Egan, a member of Ireland's most successful boyband, Westlife. Although he didn't take the crown, Jim proved to be a popular contestant.

'Appearing on "The Voice" definitely put me on the map, and it was a great period in my life,' Jim says today. 'Kian recognised the country flavour in my voice. "You're the Garth Brooks of the show," he used to say.'

Jim lives on a farm in Douglas Bridge, County Tyrone, with his wife Orlagh and their daughters, Ella and Katelyn.

He is a country boy in his heart and soul, and loves living in the countryside. 'It's a great place to bring up children,' Jim says. 'I love animals and birds, and our farm is like a zoo, with ducks and hens and Australian geese. I have a big pond as well.'

One of Jim's idols in Irish country music is Daniel O'Donnell. 'What Daniel has achieved in his career is absolutely amazing,' he acknowledges. 'Daniel really is an inspiration to all of us; even if we only get half of his success we'd be doing well.'

Jim has performed with Daniel on the TG4 show, 'Opry an Iúir'. 'I sang "Destination Donegal" with Daniel on the show, and that has been one of the highlights of my career to date, because he's an absolute legend.'

Jim with Miss Sunday World, Laura Fox.

TR Dallas

Tom Allen, aka TR Dallas, had a connection with Big Tom spanning fifty years. When he started out as a singer, TR's band was the support act for Big Tom and The Mainliners. TR also sang many of Big Tom's songs in his own show.

In 1970, at the age of nineteen, TR joined a band called The Finnavons, named after a horse that won the Grand National, in Big Tom's home town of Castleblayney.'

Life came full circle when TR joined The Mainliners in 1978, as their lead singer. Big Tom had left the band for a period at this point. 'I replaced another lead singer, John Glenn,' TR reveals.

'I don't think there is any other artist in Ireland who flew the flag for country music like Big Tom did. He really was the King of Country, and we miss his presence in the scene.'

TR Dallas has recorded two songs as a tribute to Big Tom, including 'Travelling To Big Tom', which is featured on his current album, *Be My Guest*.

'Irish songwriter PJ Murrihy wrote it after a conversation with two fans, Paddy Murray and Tom Bustin, who went all over the country four nights of the week to see Big Tom,' TR reveals.

In 1954, a cloven-hoofed devil is said to have appeared during a dance at Toreen Ballroom in County Mayo, making it one of the most famous dance halls in Ireland.

It also inspired the song 'Big Tom Doesn't Play Here Anymore', recorded by TR Dallas over thirty years ago. 'The song was written after Toreen Ballroom closed down,' TR says. 'It was a big song for me at that stage of my career. We never thought the day would come when he wouldn't be playing anywhere. We all thought Tom would be around forever.'

TR has fond memories of touring with American country legend Johnny Cash in the early days. 'Johnny was a lovely, quietly-spoken gentleman,' he remembers. 'He came into my dressing room one night, and sat down and chatted all about Ireland. He loved the simplicity of Ireland, and how people got on so well together. Johnny had his son, John Carter, and Roy Orbison's son Wesley, on the tour with him at the time.'

FACTFILE

- Tom Allen, aka TR Dallas, comes from Mount Temple, Moate, County Westmeath, and is a brother of Tony Allen of Foster & Allen.
- In the late 1960s, Tom and Tony had a band called The Prairie Boys, who played 'relief' to Big Tom and The Mainliners around the midlands.
- He teamed up with his brother Tony again in 1972, forming a new band, The Nightrunners, to support Doc Carroll and The Royal Blues.
- Tom got his major break in 1980 with the hit 'Who Shot JR Ewing?', and changed his name to TR Dallas.

Far left (from left to right): John Carter Cash, TR Dallas, Wesley Orbison, Johnny Cash.

FACTFILE

• Honky Tonk Angels are comprised of three of Ireland's top country singers: Bernie Heaney, Lorraine McDonald and CC Cooper.

• The group is the brainchild of Bernie Heaney. 'I loved CC's deep country voice, and Lorraine is the queen of harmony,' Bernie says.

• *Honky Tonk Angels* is also the title of an album by Dolly Parton, Loretta Lynn and Tammy Wynette.

• Lorraine's father, Frankie McDonald, played trumpet with the Joe Dolan band for thirty-nine years, until the singer's death.

• CC also has a strong music pedigree – her maternal grandfather, Terry Logue, was the sax player with Ireland's first showband, The Clipper Carlton.

• Bernie's great-grandfather, Bill Molloy, busked on the accordion at GAA matches around Ireland. 'My grannie died and he was left with seven children to rear, so he supported the family busking at the GAA grounds and local fairs,' she reveals.

Honky Tonk Angels

BERNIE HEANEY

Bernie says: 'I think part of the success of the Honky Tonk Angels is that we get on great, and we all have different personalities.'

Bernie reveals that the group's name came up naturally in conversation. 'When we got to know each other a little bit and were on the road individually at night, we stayed in touch by phone for company and safety. And one of us said, "We're such honky tonk angels, out in the bars and venues singing."

CC COOPER

CC Cooper is a singer with a difference – she's also a part-time nurse, in the oncology department of Dublin's Beacon Hospital. The Dublin woman says that nursing is an important part of her working week. 'I absolutely live for the music, and I feel that nursing grounds me,' CC says. 'I will travel anywhere to get up and sing a few songs, whether it's from Dublin to Donegal or to Cork.

'I see myself as having two jobs – one is about me, which is the singing, and the nursing is about what I can do for other people. I love them both, and it really balances me.'

LORRAINE MCDONALD

Their father, Frankie, introduced Lorraine and her brother Keith to live performing. She says: 'My brother Keith and myself started off playing Sunday and Wednesday jazz sessions with our dad – and when he went off touring in South Africa with Joe for six weeks, we did the gigs on our own, even though we were only thirteen and fourteen years old.'

'Dad was playing with Joe Dolan before I was born,' Lorraine points out. 'I went to see them play in ballrooms. The crowds were phenomenal, and Joe was mesmerising.'

Joe Dolan made a big impression on Lorraine in her childhood days. 'Joe always made you feel special, and at shows he'd make sure you came up to the dressing room afterwards to say hello to him.'

Keep It Country TV

Keep It Country TV is Europe's first, and only, dedicated country music television channel. It can be found on Sky 389, Freeview 87 and Freesat 516, or can be streamed live for free via www.keepitcountry.tv.

The presenters include many well-known Irish artists and personalities. Here is a flavour of what you can find on Keep It Country TV.

THE PHIL MACK INTERNATIONAL COUNTRY SHOW

The show that started it all. Phil Mack features everything from country classics through to modern-day styles, including artists from all around the globe. He reveals that Irish entertainers are the most popular with viewers of Keep It Country TV.

MARC ROBERTS

Multi-award-winning singer and songwriter Marc Roberts is also one of the stalwarts of GalwayBay FM radio.

Marc features lots of Irish artists, plus songs from the American Billboard charts, one-hit wonders from the last three decades, and a 'your song' spot, chosen by the viewers.

BROLLY & FRIENDS

Award-winning British radio presenter Bob Brolly presents his music and chat show, filmed in front of a live audience.

Part of the Ireland West music team, Michael English presents a mix of songs from his famous friends in Ireland and around the world.

Father and son Dominic and Barry Kirwan, are a winning combination with their breezy chat and tasty mix of home-grown and American country.

Other top artists and personalities picking their favourite videos include Sandy Kelly, Robert Mizzell, Lisa Stanley, John McNicholl, Gary Gamble, Kerry Fearon, Muriel O'Connor & Fran Curley, Tommy Rosney, Caitlin Murtagh, Ailish McBride, Shauna McStravock, Pamela Gilmartin, John Ryan, Michael Commins and Sarah Jory.

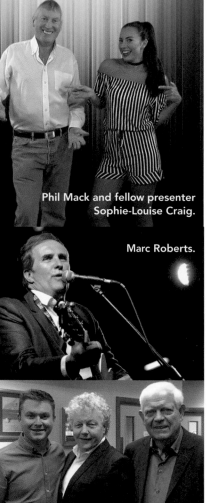

Phil Mack and fellow presenter Sophie-Louise Craig.

Marc Roberts.

Bob Brölly with Michael English and Brendan Shine.

Muriel O'Connor & Fran Curry also host their own show.

Ailish McBride.

Sandy Kelly.

HOT COUNTRY

'Hot Country', one of Europe's longest-running country music television shows, is a mix of music and interviews. Based in Cork, it's presented by Hugh O'Brien.

IRELAND WEST MUSIC TV

Hosted by Paul Claffey and Gerry Glennon and now in its sixth year, 'Ireland West Music TV' is a lively mix of Irish and American country videos and celebrity interviews.

AMERICAN COUNTRY SHOW

Award-winning radio presenter Stephen Keogh hosts the 'American Country Show', playing top US hits from the 1990s to today. There are also Irish and UK acts in the show.

AUSTRALIAN COUNTRY SHOWCASE

Music legend Frank Ifield and singer Nicki Gillis present a one-hour programme featuring Australian country music artists from today and yesteryear, with irreverent Aussie humour and banter.

THE KING SAYS COUNTRY SHOW

Hosts Eddie King and Talia LeFevre bring us the latest American country music news from www.kingsays.com and play the biggest chart-topping hits from artists such as Blake Shelton, Luke Bryan and Carrie Underwood.

LADIES OF COUNTRY

'Ladies of Country' Gemma and Marie Saunders bring a real girl-power playlist, featuring the finest country music artists from around the world, from classics to modern-day styles.

COUNTRY JAMBOREE

Hosted by Marisa D'Amato, 'Country Jamboree' plays some of the best videos from country music legends. It features a special historic country calendar segment.

Caitlin Murtagh, host of the 'Caitlin Country Music Hour'.

Phil Mack and Lisa Stanley.

Shauna McStravock.

Phil Mack with Ben Troy.

The Late Late Show

In February 2018, Dermot McEvoy, music director of the 'The Late Late Show', received a *Sunday World* All-Ireland Country Music & Entertainment Award for his support of country music on RTÉ's long-running chat show.

'Late Late' host Ryan Tubridy presented Dermot with his gong at the glittering event, staged in the Mullingar Park Hotel, County Westmeath.

Ryan himself has been a supporter of Irish country artists for many years, and hosts an annual Country Music Special, which attracts phenomenal ratings.

'We went country because it's something that the people wanted to see,' Ryan says. 'I spent ten years driving around the country for work (with RTÉ 2FM radio), and every time I got beyond certain city limits, you'd see signs going into towns saying, "Mike Denver sings here Friday night", or "Nathan Carter here Saturday, and Robert Mizzell on Sunday". I realised that country music was massive outside of the capital.'

'I realised that this is a whole world that is enormously popular, and isn't getting the love it deserves from shows like ours,' Ryan admits. 'I looked into it more and learned more, and since I got "The Late Late Show", we've been actively promoting this side of it [country music]. When I said it to Dermot [McEvoy], his response was, "You're not going to meet any resistance from me."

Ryan with Music Director Dermot McEvoy.

Sharing a joke with Patrick Feeney.

Ryan remembers the late Big Tom McBride with fondness. 'Back in the 'sixties, bands like Big Tom and The Mainliners were Ireland's version of The Beatles and the Rolling Stones,' he points out. 'For my parents' generation, they would have been the biggest thing going. I was always keen to have Big Tom on the show, and the other stars from his era – to celebrate what they achieved.'

Daniel O'Donnell acknowledges that 'The Late Late Show', its host Ryan Tubridy and music director Dermot McEvoy, have played a major role in promoting country music.

'I speak on behalf of everybody [the country artists] when I say how grateful we are to "The Late Late Show" for giving the platform to our own singers. It's a great tip of the hat to those who have entertained from the 'sixties up to now,' Daniel says.

Daniel says that singing 'Crystal Chandeliers' on the 2017 'Late Late Show' Country Special with his idol, Charley Pride, was a personal honour. 'It was a great thrill for me because I love Charley, I love his songs, I love his voice and I love the man himself,' he says. 'I sing with him as a singer, but I stand beside him as a fan.'

FACTFILE

- In his childhood days, Barry was a committed member of his school's choir. A natural-born entertainer, he loved performing in school productions and competing in various solo-singing feiseanna.
- He is an accomplished Irish dancer, having been a member of the Seamus Kerrigan School of Traditional Irish Dance from the age of five to eighteen.
- Irish dancing took him all over the country competing in the All Ireland championships, and in Scór.
- At the age of eight, Barry fell in love with drumming, going from Grade 1 to Grade 8 within five years, before going on to further study at Drumtech college in London.
- In 2010, he teamed up with his brother, Colm, in Nashville for a year, and had the honour of playing drums with American country duo Joey & Rory on four of their US shows.

Barry Kirwan

Barry Kirwan is the son of major Irish singing star Dominic Kirwan, but he says his mum, Louise, was also a big influence in his career. 'Mum was a church singer, but she was also the one who took us to all the singing feises, and she put us through our paces,' he says. 'Then any time Dad played in the area, we were taken to his shows, and I knew it was something I wanted to do. I wanted to be that guy on stage.'

Despite being passionate about country music today, Barry had a varied taste in music as a teenager, and began his musical career as a drummer in a rock band. He went to music college in London. 'I grew up loving the likes of Coldplay, and I was a rock drummer before I became a country drummer,' he says. 'Then Dad offered me a job playing drums in his band when I finished college, so that's when I began life as a country musician.'

A stint working in Nashville helped Barry to develop his skills. 'I learned a lot out there playing with American musicians,' he says. 'It was an exciting time in my young life, because I grew up listening to Garth Brooks, Vince Gill, George Strait … they were my inspiration. So to be in America performing was a thrill.'

Barry worked as a drummer with Lisa McHugh and Derek Ryan upon his return to Ireland, then finally stepped out front with his own band in 2016. 'I love it,' he says. 'The live gig is where you get the buzz. I love recording, but on stage is where you get your adrenaline pumping. You also get to meet people.'

BARRY'S FAVOURITE QUOTE

'Chase your dreams, but always know the road that'll lead you home again.'
  – Tim McGraw

Una Healy

Before she found fame in her own right, Una Healy was one of three backing singers for Brian Kennedy when he represented Ireland in the 2006 Eurovision Song Contest, performing 'Every Song Is A Cry For Love'.

'It was held in Athens, and that was another great experience,' she says of the event, in which Ireland finished tenth that year. 'I remember being nervous, even as a backing singer. Everybody suffers from nerves, but you have to use them to your advantage rather than let them destroy your performance.'

As an eleven-year-old, Una remembers watching with a sense of awe as her famous uncle, country and Irish star Declan Nerney, shot a video for his hit song 'The Marquee In Drumlish'.

'Going to gigs and chatting to Declan about the industry really inspired me,' she says. 'Every time I visited Declan in Longford, he warned me how tough the business is, but he never discouraged me.'

Una attributes her love of country music to both her mother and her uncle Declan, and says both have been big influences in her career. 'Country music was always on the radio in our home, because my mother is a big fan,' she says.

At first, Una released her own songs on an EP, and played small venues around the country. Her talent gradually began to shine through.

In 2007, she finally got her big break when she ditched her guitar and auditioned for a new British girl group. The Saturdays would become one of the most successful female acts in recent years.

'I went to the right audition at the right time, and I got into the right band. I was the only Irish member of the group, but I never for a moment felt like I didn't fit in. We were five girls chasing the same dream, doing the same thing.'

Una with hugely successful pop group The Saturdays.

FACTFILE

- The Saturdays sold over seven million records in the UK and Ireland, and are estimated to have earned £18.4 million.
- Una enjoyed a dozen Top Ten hits with The Saturdays, including 'If This Is Love', 'Up', 'Issues', 'Just Can't Get Enough', 'Forever Is Over', 'Ego', 'Missing You', 'All Fired Up' and 'What About Us' (feat Sean Paul).
- Her first solo single, 'Stay My Love', is a duet with Sam Palladio from the television show 'Nashville'.
- In 2017, Una teamed up with American country star Brett Young to record a duet of his massive single 'In Case You Didn't Know'.
- Una has two children, Aoife Bell (born 2012) and Tadhg (born 2015).

Marty Mone

Marty Mone from Monaghan has enjoyed a string of novelty hits with songs like 'Hit The Diff', 'Slip The Clutch' and 'Better Than A Dream'. The agricultural contractor and trucker has a style of his own.

At the age of eighteen, Marty was working full-time driving tractors, diggers and lorries, while also gigging with a band at the weekends. Then he began writing and recording songs and making his own music videos.

Marty's career took off when he penned 'Hit The Diff', and the video went viral on YouTube. It led to Marty performing at Croke Park, the SSE Arena in Belfast, on the 'Late Late Show' and at the National Ploughing Championships. He also wrote 'The Ploughing Song', which was used in the television advert for the 2017 Ploughing Championships.

His song 'Slip The Clutch', about lorries and the trucking life, also proved to be a smash hit with fans, and spurred the singer on to record a full album, called *Hit The Diff*. Another hit, 'Better Than A Dream', has become a popular first-dance song at weddings.

Marty was injured in June 2018 while filming a stunt for one of his songs on a quad bike. He suffered a fractured shoulder, and was left concussed. Mone was on his own at the time, and doesn't remember much about the incident, but he said the fact that he was wearing a helmet saved him from serious injury. He has made a full recovery.

Shane Owens

Born in Reading outside London, to Irish parents from County Cavan, Shane Owens fell in love with Irish country music as a child.

'I would raid my dad's record collection, and listen for endless hours to Mick Flavin, Mike Denver and some legends from the USA, including Waylon Jennings, George Jones and Willie Nelson,' Shane says.

By the age of five, Shane was performing the classic song 'Country Roads' on stage at his local Irish club.

In 2014, Shane entered a 'Search for a Star' contest in Ireland, and he emerged a winner out of the 500 wannabes who participated in the event.

The contest, run by local radio presenter and country music promoter Joe Finnegan, helped to establish Shane's career in Ireland.

'It's an absolute dream come true to be doing what I'm doing,' Shane says. 'I love performing and seeing people smile. There's no greater feeling than looking out on to the dance floor and seeing that people are enjoying your music. I particularly love Irish country, because you can really dance to it and it has that special feel to it.'

Ireland has always been a home from home for Shane, as all his school holidays were spent in Cavan with his parents. The young singer has moved to Cavan, and has put down roots in the country since launching his career as a country singer. 'I knew I had to live in Ireland, whether it was to sing or not. I've known this since I was about twelve,' he says.

Country Style — Lisa McHugh

Performing on stage gives Lisa McHugh plenty of opportunity to indulge her passion for fashion. 'There's not many girls who need an excuse to get dolled up, and I get to do it every day when I'm working,' Lisa admits.

'Most people would notice a change in my style over the last three years. I like to change my "look" as much as I possibly can. I don't want it to be repetitive, and I like to have fun.'

IF FANS WANT TO GET THE COUNTRY 'LOOK' FOR FESTIVALS, WHAT SHOULD THEY BE WEARING?

'There are certain elements of clothing that will always be relevant to country. They include denim shorts and a wee denim jacket and checked shirt, or flowery dresses and cowboy boots.'

WHAT IS THE LISA MCHUGH 'LOOK'?

'I like elegant, I like classy, but I like "bold" as well. What I wear depends on my mood, and it depends on the event and the audience.'

LISA'S ACCESSORIES

'I love bling. I always have glitzy jewellery on stage. My favourite range would be Swarovski, but they can be very expensive, so I don't buy them all the time. You can't beat the likes of River Island and Top Shop for glitzy costume jewellery. I'm a nightmare with jewellery, because I'm always losing stuff. That's why I tend to go for high street jewellery that doesn't cost a lot.'

LISA'S PERSONAL TOP THREE OUTFITS

• 'One of my favourite outfits is the gold-and-silver jumpsuit I wore for the performance in my live DVD. It was very different to anything I had worn before. I found it online, and it's by Michael Costello. His clothes have been worn by Celine Dion, Beyoncé, Meghan Trainor, Lady Gaga and Alicia Keys.'

• 'My second choice would be the black trouser suit I wore at the "Late Late Show" Country Music Special this year [2018]. It was classy and it also pushed the boundaries. I picked it up in The Dolls House Fashion Boutique in England.'

• 'I loved my casual, floral, girlie dress from Harry & George Boutique in Enniskillen that I wore for my song "Girl With A Fishing Rod", when I sang it on the "Late Late Show" this year [2018]. After my "Late Late Show" appearance went up online, that outfit sold out in the shop within half an hour!'

• While Lisa is first and foremost a singer, her sense of style is compelling, and she likes to keep fans up to date on Instagram and other social media platforms.

• 'I find that if I don't tag the outfits, I'm going to get people asking where they're from,' she says. 'So now when I put up a picture, I tag the source of the outfit.'

Country Style — Cliona Hagan

GET THE LOOK

'Denim on denim, which I love myself, is very popular on the country music scene. You see fans wearing little summer dresses with cute, wee denim frilly jackets. Denim or leather jackets are definitely part of the "look". A little summer dress with ankle boots and a nice, flared jacket has a country feel to it. Denim jeans and tops are good too. The country "look" is a casual one.'

THESE BOOTS ARE MADE FOR DANCING

'Within the country scene, you notice a lot more little ankle boots than you do stilettos. Boots are always associated with country music, but the ankle boots are very stylish.

'When it comes to dancing, they are more comfortable as well. After one or two dances in a row wearing stilettos, your feet are sore and you can't keep up with the beat of the music. Ankle boots are also more practical for festivals, where the dance floors can be uneven.'

'My outfits come from Crystal Boutique in Armagh. They have a fabulous range of clothes, and they are my sponsor.

'For my stage gear, it's fun to have a little bit of glitz and glamour. Sparkly tops and sequins always catch the light.

'My main objective on the stage is to feel comfortable, and to wear an outfit that represents me and the style that I like. I'm not one to show too much leg. I like to dress down casual, but when I'm attending awards shows I'll wear something more formal and classy.'

'For me as a stage performer, fashion is very, very vital.'

HEALTH

'I go to the gym as much as possible, and I watch what I eat. I don't eat much junk, because it's so vital to be healthy. As an entertainer, working and travelling at night, my sleeping pattern is all over the place. I try not to eat late at night. My personal rule is not to eat after 6.30pm. That's the time when I'd be craving for something sweet, so I fill the gap with a cup of coffee or tea, and I drink a lot of water to satisfy the yearning.

'I take a lot of Vitamin C as well, because I don't get enough daylight at times, and I eat lots of fruit. This is probably the most unhealthy job you can have, so you have to make sure that you counteract it with a good health regime.'

GET THE CLIONA LOOK

• A little skirt, ankle boots, and long-sleeved top.
• Little summer dresses – 'I think they are really cute' – complemented by a little leather jacket.

FACTFILE

- Olivia's musical journey began at the age of five, when she discovered the tin whistle. From there, she progressed to the button accordion, playing at numerous Fleadh Cheoils around Ireland.

- Her family run a bar, Tom's Tavern, in the small town of Ferbane, and Olivia regularly performed with the bands who played there. 'My first stage appearance was in the pub,' she says.

- The Philomena Begley version of the Billie Jo Spears classic, 'Blanket On The Ground', was the first country song Olivia learned and sang.

- Michael English, Robert Mizzell, Sandy Kelly, Gerry Guthrie, Matt Leavy and Simon Casey are among the stars who performed at the launch of her new album, *Forever Country*.

Olivia Douglas

Since first gaining national recognition as a contestant on TG4's 'Glór Tíre' in early 2016, Olivia Douglas, from Ferbane, County Offaly, has become a major attraction.

Olivia is a female singer with a difference – she also plays the accordion as part of her act.

'The accordion was always in the family, on my father's side,' she says. 'My great-granny played it, my granny played it, and my father played it. I even have an accordion that was owned by my great-granny, and it's my treasure.'

Olivia was mentored on 'Glór Tíre' by Irish country legend Sandy Kelly.

'I grew up listening to Sandy Kelly's music. I never thought that one day I'd be duetting with her on a TV show, singing "Good Hearted Woman",' Olivia says.

'It was a real honour to be working with Sandy, and she put me at ease straight away. She's a lovely, warm person and, my God, she has great stories from her days in the business, working and recording with Johnny Cash.'

Olivia had to come to terms quickly with working on a major television show. 'I went from singing in our family pub in County Offaly to performing in front of cameras, so that was a challenge. But I got through it, and I realised then that this is what I want to do as a career.'

So what is life like on the road? 'Well, most of the time is spent in my car,' Olivia says. 'You live out of a car in this business. There are always bags of clothes in the car, but it's great to have a busy life. It's a tough life as a girl, but if you love it, you'll keep plugging away at it.'

2018 saw Olivia performing on the *Sunday World* Stage at Dublin's 3Arena, during the three-day Country to Country festival that featured a host of American superstars, including Tim McGraw and Faith Hill.

Keelan

Keelan Arbuckle is a teen sensation from Burnfoot, County Donegal. For the last couple of years he has been studying for his Leaving Cert by day, and performing with his four-piece band at night. 'There were times when I didn't get home till four or five in the morning, then I'd be up at 7.30am for school,' he reveals.

Keelan got his big break when he posted videos on Facebook of himself performing. 'A manager called Steve Bloor spotted them and messaged me, asking if I had any professionally recorded songs. I then recorded "That's Important To Me", "Callin' Baton Rouge", "Amarillo By Morning" and "Diana". Steve was impressed enough to become my manager, and I have now formed my own band.'

Songwriting is one of Keelan's passions. 'A song I released, called "My Guitar", is one I wrote myself, and it has been very successful. Farmers love their tractors, and I love my guitar,' he says. 'Up to now, I have had five number one singles on iTunes, and was voted "Newcomer of the Year" at the Hot Country TV awards in 2016.'

FACTFILE
• Keelan developed an interest in music from a very young age, when he would sit and watch his grandfather singing and playing the accordion.
• When he was nine, Keelan asked his parents for a guitar, and began music lessons.
• Keelan's first big success was winning a school competition called Pop Goes Primary.
• Keelan has achieved every country singer's dream, by performing on stage at the Grand Ole Opry while visiting the venue.

Lee Matthews

Lee Matthews started out on the international pop scene as a teenager in boyband Streetwize.

Then he moved on to a new group called Access All Areas, who were offered a million-pound deal by Warner in the UK.

'Then one of the band members decided he didn't want to pursue his pop career anymore – and the entire deal fell through,' Lee reveals.

Lee's heart has always been in country. 'What I really wanted to do from the very start was to sing in a country band like Rascal Flatts,' he says.

'When I was in a pop group, I realised what I was missing as I listened to great country artists on the radio every day,' he says. 'Now I'm just so delighted to be a part of the Irish country music scene.'

Lee's mother Veronica, who had performed in showbands, encouraged her son to change direction and move into country music.

'I had the impression that country was for an older scene, but Mum started telling me about this young guy called Nathan Carter,' he reveals.

'One night I went to see him perform in the Allingham Arms Hotel in Bundoran, and I couldn't believe how different the country scene was to what I remembered when I was a kid.'

FACTFILE
- Lee Matthews was just eight years old when he first performed on stage with Daniel O'Donnell.
- At the age of eleven, Lee represented Ireland in the World Championships of Performing Arts in Los Angeles.
- Lee is a doting dad to his son, Noah.

Niamh Lynn

Originally from Dublin's Castleknock and now living in Mullagh, County Cavan, Niamh Lynn channels the female legends of American country music – Patsy Cline, Tammy Wynette, Loretta Lynn and Billie Jo Spears – in her performances.

'They are songs that people don't sing anymore, but I knew there was an audience out there for them, as those songs bring back a lot of memories to some people,' she says.

Niamh has also established her own image on the scene through her love of 'fifties-era dresses and outfits. 'I buy them online,' she reveals. 'I love them, and they cover a multitude.'

Her album, *An Old Fashioned Song*, is a tribute to the American ladies of country who have inspired her.

PATSY CLINE

'I grew up listening to Patsy Cline. My nan, Nanny Wynne, used to play her all the time. I think that's where I get my singing style from, because I used to mimic Patsy as a kid.'

TAMMY WYNETTE

'I read a book on Tammy, and was inspired by how she lived her life, and how she was determined to be a successful artist as well as being a mother.'

LORETTA LYNN

'Loretta Lynn's life story is also remarkable, because she grew up in an era when it was so difficult for women to make a life of their own and to achieve success. She married at fifteen and had kids. But Loretta was a strong woman who didn't take any nonsense off anybody.'

BILLIE JO SPEARS

'I came across Billie Jo Spears through the song "Sing Me An Old Fashioned Song", which I recorded. "Sing Me An Old Fashioned Song" did really well for me; it has had nearly two million hits.'

Four legends of American country music (top to bottom): Patsy Cline, Tammy Wynette, Loretta Lynn and Billie Jo Spears.

The Record Producer
(Jonathan Owens)

Record producer Jonathan Owens, working in his Spout Studio in Longford, is the studio wizard behind some of Irish country music's biggest hits, including Nathan Carter's 'Wagon Wheel'.

Jonathan's parents, Chuck and June Owens, were country singers, and he grew up surrounded by major stars from Larry Cunningham and Big Tom to Daniel O'Donnell. 'My dad was also a record producer, and that's where I got the bug,' he reveals.

WHAT ARE YOUR CHILDHOOD MEMORIES?

'I remember being on the road with my parents, and how they used to bring me up on stage to play the drums when I was five or six years of age as a feature in their show.'

HOW DID YOU GET INTO THE RECORDING BUSINESS?

'I first joined Declan Nerney's band as a drummer at the age of seventeen, and I spent nine years in his band. I then left Declan's band for two years, to concentrate on recording work. I went back on the road with Mike Denver for six months, and then Jimmy Buckley's band for two years, before going full-time into studio work.'

WAS IT DIFFICULT TO GET SINGERS TO RECORD WITH YOU?

'I was lucky that they all trusted me, because I had a history in the business, even though I was still a young guy. Singers and musicians would always say to me, "I remember you when you were only this height."'

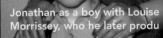
Jonathan as a boy with Louise Morrissey, who he later produ

WHO HAVE YOU WORKED WITH?

'I've worked with them all, with the exception of Daniel O'Donnell, who has his own producer, John Ryan. But I've recorded Larry Cunningham and Big Tom, right up to contemporary artists like Patrick Feeney, Robert Mizzell and Jimmy Buckley.'

DID YOU REALISE 'WAGON WHEEL' WAS GOING TO BE A MASSIVE HIT WHEN YOU RECORDED IT WITH NATHAN CARTER?

'I don't think either of us did. I wouldn't have thought of it being a country single. It was a toss-up between recording "Wagon Wheel" and another song, but we both felt it was great. The local radio stations weren't too sure about it, but when it got into the night clubs and the jukeboxes, everybody in the country was singing, "rock me mama". It just grew and grew.'

WHAT DID THE SUCCESS OF 'WAGON WHEEL' DO FOR YOUR CAREER?

'"Wagon Wheel" opened a lot of people's ears in the business to what I was doing. I was now "the guy who recorded and produced 'Wagon Wheel'". On the back of it, I got Derek Ryan and Lisa McHugh.'

CAN A RECORD PRODUCER GUARANTEE A SONG IS GOING TO BE A SMASH HIT?

'It's the public who decide what's a hit. I can produce a great song today, give it 100 percent and put the best into it. It's like baking a cake, you get the best ingredients and mix it up.

'Then you hand it over to the fans, and they ultimately decide whether they like it or not.'

Jonathan with Charley Pride.

(Left to right): Rose and Tom McBride, Margo, Jonathan.

The Videographer
(Michael Bracken)

Nothing brings a song to life and promotes it better than a creative, high-quality music video. Today, with social media, videos are an even more essential promotional tool.

Country music videographer Michael Bracken (Bracken Entertainment), from Mullingar, County Westmeath, has been the go-to man for all the major artists for the last three decades, and has recorded more than 1,300 country music videos.

Michael's YouTube channel, BrackenEntertainment.com, has a combined total of over four million views.

HOW DID YOU GET INTO THE BUSINESS?

'I bought my first little camcorder when I was eighteen years old. It cost me £1,700, and took me four years to pay back. I started doing football matches, motor rallies, first communions and weddings.

Then Mick Clerkin of Ritz Records gave me the chance to do a full fourteen-track DVD for John Hogan, when I knew nothing about music. I started working with Foster & Allen twenty-two years ago, and I've done all their videos since then.'

IS IT EXPENSIVE TO MAKE A VIDEO?

'A video at the moment will cost anything from €1,000 to €3,000, depending on how many days you put into it, and how long you want to spend on the edit. There are cheap videos out there that are deplorable and don't do the singer justice.

'I would advise every singer or band to spend the extra bit of money and get a professional to do their video. If you go to the main TV stations and you don't have a top-quality product, they won't show it.'

HOW LONG DOES IT TAKE TO MAKE A VIDEO?

'You need to do a prep two to three weeks in advance, then film for two days, then an edit for three to four days. When I'm doing a Foster & Allen video, for three-and-a-half minutes it's seven days' work.'

WHAT IS YOUR PERSONAL FAVOURITE VIDEO?

Because I grew up in the country, the nearest to my heart is the TR Dallas song "This Story I Tell You Is True". Growing up, I experienced all the old traditions and ways of life that are featured in that video.'

DO THE SINGERS FIND IT DIFFICULT TO ACT IN VIDEOS?

'Of course they need guidance, but I've found the majority of them to be natural performers in front of the camera. I keep on repeating shots until I'm happy. Mick Foster calls me "one more!", because I'll always look for an extra shot.'

WHAT IS NATHAN CARTER LIKE TO WORK WITH?

'I started off working with Nathan seven years ago, and I have to say, it's always great craic. I did Nathan's very first video, for a song called "One For The Road", and I went on to do songs like "Caledonia", "Good Morning Beautiful", "Temple Bar and "Burning Bridges", featuring Foster & Allen with Nathan.'

Ciarán Rosney

Ciarán comes from Dernagun, County Offaly, but now lives in Latton, Castleblayney. 'I started playing with my brothers in a band from about the age of thirteen,' he says.

'Later, I had a two-piece with my older brother Stephen, and I got to know how to perform and learned what songs worked. It was always a bit of a hobby when I was in school, as I never had the guts to go full-time. But now is my time.'

Married with two young daughters, Ciaran pays tribute to his wife, Jean, for supporting his ambition. 'Without her, I wouldn't be able to do what I'm doing,' he says.

'I've travelled the country as a solo performer, performing at social dances, in pubs and clubs and anywhere that would have me,' Ciarán says. 'Finally, I reached the point where I felt I had enough of a following to put a band on the road.'

'I'm an old-style country singer,' Ciarán points out. 'I'm now singing songs that I grew up with, songs that my parents were singing.'

FACTFILE
• As a child, Ciarán won tickets to a Declan Nerney show when he sang 'The Marquee In Drumlish' on Shannonside radio. Declan Nerney invited Ciarán up on stage to sing the track with him at the live show.
• Ciarán did his bachelor degree in music in Waterford, specialising in classical guitar; and he studied for his Masters in music technology with John Feehily in the College of Music in Dublin.
• A music teacher for many years, he taught in colleges in Maynooth and Dundalk.

Ben Troy

THE WEE AMIGOS

Ben Troy first made an impact nationally when he performed on 'The Late Late Show' as a member of The Wee Amigos.

'We did all right as The Wee Amigos. But eventually we grew up and grew out of it, and went our separate ways. It was a great experience; I wouldn't change a thing about it.'

BY GEORGE, IT'S THE GRAND OLE OPRY

At the age of seventeen, Ben achieved every country singer's dream of singing on stage at Nashville's famous Grand Ole Opry.

'I went to Nashville in 2015, on a tour organised by Phil Mack,' Ben reveals. 'The George Jones Museum had just opened. Lisa Stanley, who was recording a TV show, was chatting to Nancy Jones, the widow of George Jones. Lisa introduced me to Nancy, saying, "This fella sings."

'Nancy said to me, "Do you sing some Cash?" I told her I did. So she asked me to sing for her. We then went up to a rooftop bar, where there was a band and about 200 people, and on the way up in the elevator, she asked me, "Do you sing some George Jones?"

'I asked her what her favourite George Jones song was, and she said, "He Stopped Loving Her Today". So I got up on stage and sang it for her. The next night she had me singing on the stage at the Grand Ole Opry!

'That was a phenomenal experience. It was like somebody pressing the accelerator, and it didn't stop. Nancy is an absolute lady, and I'm still in contact with her.'

Paul Kelly

Paul Kelly comes from the small village of Pettigo in County Donegal. 'My first real memory of performing was when I was about nine and I was asked to take part in a local talent competition,' he recalls. 'I enjoyed every second of being on stage, and it made it even better when I won.

'Then, when I was twelve, I started playing in a two-piece band with my mother, a few nights a week. That was a brilliant time, as I was doing what I loved and getting paid for it.'

Paul, a multi-instrumentalist, went on to play in several groups before launching his own six-piece outfit, comprised of some of Ireland's top musicians.

'I haven't looked back since,' he says. 'The response from the promoters and dancers has been amazing.'

Paul has enjoyed a string of country hits with original songs like 'So In Love', 'The Hooley', 'The Hangover', 'Willie The Dealer', 'Tang's Hauling', 'Summertime', 'On The Market' and 'Cut The Grass'.

'Although I played all kinds of music, country has always had a special place in my heart,' he says. 'My neighbour, Andy Cox, told me he had written a few country songs, and was interested in working with me on them. The very first song that came to be was "So In Love". It became a major hit straight away.'

One of the highlights of Paul's career to date, he says, has been recording the duet 'Lost Love', also written by Andy Cox, with country music royalty Georgette Jones, the daughter of American legends George Jones and Tammy Wynette.

Trudi Lalor

Trudi Lalor has been honoured with gongs for 'Female Vocalist of the Year' and 'Female Entertainer of the Year'. One of eleven children from Mountrath, County Laois, Trudi has been a stalwart of the Irish country music scene over three decades. Her path to a music career began in school musicals and local talent contests, as well as singing at church weddings and in local concerts.

When Louise Morrissey was seriously injured in a head-on crash while travelling to a concert in September 1993, Trudi, then an up-and-coming singer, stepped in to front Louise's band and fulfil all her Irish and UK tour commitments. After six months recuperating, Louise returned to the band, and Trudi went on to become an artist in her own right.

Trudi's husband and manager Billy Morrissey, a brother of singer Louise, has composed several of her signature songs, including 'Beautiful Isle Of Somewhere' (a duet with her late mother), 'These Are The Good Old Days' and 'Old Friends Are Best'.

Trudi presents her own Sunday morning show, 'Premier Country', on Tipp FM radio. She has interviewed her own musical heroes for the show, including Shane MacGowan, who, although born in England, grew up in Tipperary.

Trudi revealed that when she arrived at Shane's house to do the interview, there was no phone signal, so she had to climb over his gate. As she was walking up the avenue towards Shane's house, her mobile rang as the signal was restored. It was Shane Mac-Gowan, telling her where to find the key to let herself in!

Opry le Daniel

TG4 plays a major role in promoting country music in Ireland, through shows like the talent contest 'Glór Tíre'. Their 'Opry' entertainment series is also hugely popular, now called 'Opry le Daniel' and presented by Daniel O'Donnell.

The 'Opry' show is now in its eighth series. The current run features international stars such as Charley Pride and Rita Coolidge, alongside Ireland's top performers and emerging talent.

'Opry le Daniel' boss Philip McGovern says: 'We have a great mix of International and Irish artists. Plus, we feature lots of unique TV moments, where we get families, like Brendan Quinn and his family, or the Kirwans and the Ryans, to play together, or artists to pay tributes to the likes of Jim Reeves or Johnny Cash.'

'Country music has been on the up in recent years, and we have been growing with it,' Philip says. 'We were the first to feature Nathan Carter. We did a full show with him way back at the start, and he has kind of grown up with the show. Then a whole new wave of people, like Derek Ryan, came behind Nathan.'

'What I love about doing "Opry" is seeing something magical happening, like the Kirwan family – Dominic and his sons Colm and Barry – coming together and producing an amazing performance. It was like watching a Las Vegas show; they "owned" that stage, and it was fantastic to see. It was the same with Derek Ryan's family and Brendan Quinn's family. What they all did together made great TV, and the audiences loved them.'

The current series of 'Opry le Daniel' was recorded in front of a live audience, at the Millennium Forum in Derry. 'People coming to a live show expect something special. We try to create "moments" that are going to be memorable, like Daniel singing *as Gaeilge* or doing duets with the other stars, such as Charley Pride or Georgette Jones, the daughter of George Jones and Tammy Wynette. They are special moments you won't see anywhere else.'

Daniel O'Donnell says: 'What I love about doing the "Opry" shows is that it gives a platform to country music. In order for country music to continue to grow and for new talent to flourish, it needs the support of radio and television.

'When people see the talent that is on offer, it brings them out to the dances and concerts. We have great young country music artists in Ireland, and shows like our "Opry" series really benefit them.'

Below (left to right): Matt Leavy, Patrick Feeney, Daniel, Isla Grant, Al Grant and Tony Kerr, at a Jim Reeves tribute night on Opry le Daniel.

Robert Mizzell, Georgette Jones and Jimmy Buckley.

James Quinn, Daniel, Charley Pride,
Brendan Quinn and Stephen Quinn.

Gloria

Known simply as Gloria, Gloria Sherry (*nee* Smyth) holds the record for the biggest Irish hit of all time, with the classic 'One Day At A Time'.

The eldest of nine children from Navan, County Meath, Gloria's first experience on stage was dancing and playing accordion with her father's group, The Arcadians Showband, at the age of ten. After leaving school, Gloria found work as a piano player, eventually joining the Maurice Lynch Showband as a singer in the late 1960s.

Gloria toured around Ireland, singing alongside Johnny McEvoy, in the early to mid-1970s, before breaking out on her own with her band, Mississippi.

Gloria's brother, Jimmy Smyth, is widely regarded as one of Ireland's greatest guitarists. He formed The Bogey Boys in 1978, and two years later had U2 as a support band in the Cork Opera House. He has also played with Van Morrison, Tony Childs, Roger Daltrey, Chaka Khan, Lisa Stansfield and Gilbert O'Sullivan. A Grammy-nominated artist, he played at the Grammy Awards in 1988 and 1996.

Gloria released her version of the song 'One Day At A Time' in August 1977, reaching number five in the Irish charts. However, when Gloria re-released it the following year, she scored a number one hit, remaining in the charts for ninety-seven weeks, throughout the whole of 1979 and into 1980 – the longest run for any single in Irish chart history.

Left: Gloria with Brian Coll.

Louise Morrissey

Louise Morrissey, a native of Bansha, County Tipperary, is celebrating thirty years in the country music scene as a solo artist, having started on her own in 1988.

Louise's career began at the age of fourteen with her brothers, Billy and Norman, as part of folk group The Morrisseys, whose hits included 'The Old Rustic Bridge By The Mill' and 'Sweet Forget-Me-Not'. They regularly toured Ireland, the UK and Canada.

When the Irish country music scene lost its 'King', Big Tom McBride, this year, there was an outpouring of grief and sadness.

'Big Tom is one of the first country artists I listened to as a young girl,' she recalls. 'My family had his albums, the old vinyl LPs, in our home.

'Tom had the type of following where people stopped dancing, and stopped everything, when he appeared on stage. He was a lovely man to meet, very pleasant and a gentle giant, really.'

'Nowadays, my main work is doing guest spots at shows,' Louise says. 'I enjoy working this way, because it means I don't have the responsibility of keeping a band on the road.'

When she's not performing on stage, Louise enjoys life down on the farm at New Inn, County Tipperary. 'Johnny, my husband, is a farmer, and I love the lifestyle,' she says.

Daniel O'Donnell is a close friend and supporter of Louise, who had a big hit early in her career with a song called 'The Night Daniel O'Donnell Came To Town'. 'I worked with him on various shows through the years, and he's an absolute gentleman,' she reveals.

Sandy Kelly

Sandy Kelly, a native of Sligo, was born into the Duskey showbiz family, who travelled the country, putting on shows in small towns and villages. 'My dad would travel ahead and put up the poster, and it looked like "The Greatest Show On Earth",' she laughs.

'Sometimes people would pay with food rather than money, and it was gladly accepted. I remember eggs, potatoes and fish being handed over at the door.'

Sandy grew up to be a singer, performing as Sandy Duskey and The Fairways, and later as the Duskey Sisters, with her sister Barbara and cousin Nina. They represented Ireland in the 1982 Eurovision Song Contest with 'Here Today, Gone Tomorrow'.

Sandy will never forget the call she received from 'The Man In Black', Johnny Cash. The singer had just finished an interview with an Irish radio station, promoting her cover of the Patsy Cline classic, 'Crazy'.

At that moment in 1989, Johnny Cash happened to be on tour in Ireland, heading for a show in Omagh, and he heard Sandy's song on the car radio. 'I thought it was somebody winding me up when he rang the station to speak to me,' Sandy recalls. 'But it was Johnny on the line, and he invited me to his show in Omagh that night. When I got there, Johnny had another surprise in store for me – I was to support him, singing Patsy Cline songs with his band.'

Sandy Kelly with her son, bluegrass musician Willie Kelly

It was the start of a friendship between the Irish star and the American country icon that lasted until his death in 2003. 'Before I knew it, I was in Johnny Cash's house in Nashville, hanging out with all his friends,' Sandy says.

Sandy and Johnny Cash recorded a duet, 'Woodcarver', which gave her another huge hit. 'My career took off so fast after meeting Johnny Cash, I hadn't time to think about it,' she says.

Tours of America followed, and Sandy had her own hugely popular series on RTÉ television for three years running, with the highlight being her Patsy Cline segment in each show. 'I was on the road to realising all my dreams; it was a wonderful part of my life,' she says.

She remembers Johnny Cash as a humble man, with a great sense of humour.

'Johnny was always playing child-like games when I was on the road with him and June and the other Carter sisters, Helen and Anita,' she recalls.

When Johnny died, Sandy sang with his family and friends at the graveside. 'It was a modest and humble funeral, just like the man himself,' she recalls.

Sandy starred in a show dedicated to Patsy Cline, which was a huge hit abroad. 'Patsy Cline has been good to me,' Sandy says. 'Oh my God, I'd have starved to death if it wasn't for Patsy. She kept my career going.'

Brendan Shine

When 'X Factor' presenter Dermot O'Leary published his memoir, *The Soundtrack to My Life*, in 2014, he styled the book around songs that had made an impact on him. And number one on Dermot's list from his childhood was Brendan Shine's hit 'Catch Me If You Can'.

He says it was always on his Wexford parents' record player on Sunday nights, when they would hold impromptu céilís.

Shine sprang a surprise on O'Leary at his book launch in Eason's of O'Connell Street, Dublin, in November 2014. He turned up at the event, and sang 'Catch Me If You Can' for the 'X Factor' star.

Brendan Shine has been a folk and country star for more than fifty years, with novelty hits like 'Do You Want Your Oul Lobby Washed Down', 'Catch Me If You Can', 'Carrots From Clonown' and 'Doogeens'.

'I started with my dad, playing in a little two-piece, and then I joined a professional céilí band in 1963,' Brendan recalls. 'Those bands used to sit down and drink and smoke when they were playing. They were so far removed from the entertainment of today.

'The céilí scene was pretty tough, because the showbands were all the rage at the time. But it was a great training ground, and it set me up for the road.'

At the start of his career, Brendan, a native of Roscommon, juggled life as a touring musician with his day job as a carrot farmer. Looking back, he says: 'I'd get home at seven in the morning, in the ice and the snow, and then I'd get back into a van and drive up to the Dublin fruit and veg market with the carrots. I'd be in the market at six o'clock, after coming back from a céilí.'

Brendan originally made his name as an accordionist, before taking up singing. In 1971, he had a number one hit with 'O'Brien Has No Place To Go', which stayed in the charts for five months.

'The showbands were doing the English and American pop hits, and I came along with original songs like "O'Brien Has No Place To Go", "Where The Three Counties Meet" and "Abbeyshule",' he recalls.

His hit, 'Do You Want Your Oul Lobby Washed Down', stayed at number one for six weeks in 1979.

Despite a high-flying career as an entertainer, Brendan remained close to his roots and has been blessed with a happy family life. 'I led a normal life as near as I could,' he says. 'I continued on farming and I sang in the choir of our local church. I got married [to Kathleen] at twenty-four, and I have two daughters [Emily and Philippa], and now grandchildren.'

Brendan with his daughter Philippa.

Mary Duff

Mary Duff has been Daniel O'Donnell's touring partner since 1987.

Mary was a contestant in the *Sunday World* Search For A Star competition, and Daniel's manager, Sean Reilly, happened to be in the audience that night. Afterwards, Sean invited her to audition for Daniel's show.

'Sean asked me that night if I would be interested in doing support for Daniel, and I agreed to go for an audition,' she reveals.

Daniel loved Mary's style of performing, and the pair hit it off immediately.

Mary is still a hugely popular member of Daniel's touring show. 'We're very lucky that our voices blend really well together,' Mary says. 'And we know each other that well now, we don't have to think about it; we look at each other, and we know how the phrasing is going.'

It was Mary's late mother who first introduced her to Daniel's music. 'My mother actually heard him before I did,' she says. 'She said to me, "Oh, you should hear this young singer – he's great." Daniel was being played on all the pirate radio stations at the time.'

Mary works as a solo artist whenever Daniel takes time off. She tours the UK, Switzerland and Australia, where she is popular in her own right. Her critically acclaimed solo albums include *Voice Of An Angel*, recorded with the Prague Philharmonic Orchestra.

Reflecting on her career with Daniel, Mary admits she sometimes has to pinch herself. 'With Daniel, I've gone to places I never dreamed of going,' she says.

Mary with Majella O'Donnell.